WordPerfect 6 for Windows
The Visual Learning Guide

Watch for these forthcoming titles in this series:

Quicken 3 for Windows: The Visual Learning Guide

Available Now!

Windows 3.1: The Visual Learning Guide
Excel 4 for Windows: The Visual Learning Guide
Word for Windows 6: The Visual Learning Guide
WordPerfect 6 for DOS: The Visual Learning Guide
WordPerfect 6 for Windows: The Visual Learning Guide
1-2-3 for Windows: The Visual Learning Guide

How to Order:

Quantity discounts are available from the publisher, Prima Publishing, P.O. Box 1260BK, Rocklin, CA 95677; FAX (916) 786-0488. On your letterhead include information concerning the intended use of the books and the number of books you wish to purchase.

WordPerfect 6
for Windows
The Visual Learning Guide

Grace Joely Beatty, Ph.D.

David C. Gardner, Ph.D.

Prima Publishing
P.O. Box 1260BK
Rocklin, CA 95677

Library of Congress Catalog Card Number: 91-39566
ISBN: 1-55958-396-7

Executive Editor: Roger Stewart
Managing Editor: Neweleen A. Trebnik
Project Manager: Becky Freeman
Production and Layout: Marian Hartsough Associates
Interior Design: Grace Joely Beatty, S. Linda Beatty, David C. Gardner,
   Laurie Stewart, and Kim Bartusch
Technical Editing: Linda Miles
Cover Design: Page Design, inc.
Color Separations: Ocean Quigley
Index: Katherine Stimson

Prima Publishing
Rocklin, CA 95677-1260

93 94 95 96 RRD 10 9 8 7 6 5 4 3 2 1

Printed in the United States of America

Acknowledgments

We are deeply indebted to reviewers around the country who gave generously of their time to test every step in the manuscript. David Coburn, Ray Holder, Jeannie Jones, and David Sauer cannot be thanked enough!

Carolyn Holder and Anne-Barbara Norris are our in-house production team, reviewers, proofreaders, screen capturers, and friends. We could not possibly do what we do without them. They along with Margaret Short keep us functioning.

We are personally and professionally delighted to work with everyone at Prima Publishing, especially Roger Stewart, executive editor, Neweleen Trebnik, managing editor, Becky Freeman, project manager, Debbie Parisi, publicity coordinator, and Kim Bartusch, production coordinator.

Linda Miles, technical editor, Ocean Quigley, color separator, Marian Hartsough, Linda Hart, and Barbara Lewis, interior layout, and Paul Page, cover design, contributed immensely to the final product.

Bill Gladstone and Matt Wagner of Waterside Productions created the idea for this series. Their faith in us has never wavered.

Joseph and Shirley Beatty made this series possible. We can never repay them.

Asher Shapiro has always been there when we needed him.

Paula Gardner Capaldo and David Capaldo have been terrific. Thanks, Joshua and Jessica, for being such wonderful kids! Our project humorist, Mike Bumgardner, always came through when we needed a boost!

We could not have met the deadlines without the technical support of Ray Holder, our electrical genius, Fred Harper of Blue Line Communications, Inc., our computer genius, and Sandi Hetzel of WordPerfect Corporation and the outstanding WordPerfect technical support staff. Thank you all!

Contents at a Glance

CONTENTS

Customize Your Learning

Prima Visual Learning Guides are not like any other computer books you have ever seen. They are based on our years in the classroom, our corporate consulting, and our research at Boston University on the best ways to teach technical information to nontechnical learners. Most important, this series is based on the feedback of a panel of reviewers from across the country who range in computer knowledge from "panicked at the thought" to sophisticated.

This is not an everything-you've-ever-wanted-to-know-about WordPerfect 6 for Windows book. It is designed to give you the information you need to perform basic (and some not so basic) functions with confidence and skill. It is a book that our reviewers claim makes it "really easy" for anyone to learn WordPerfect 6 for Windows quickly.

Each chapter is illustrated with full-color screens to guide you through every task. The combination of screens, step-by-step instructions, and pointers make it impossible for you to get lost or confused as you follow along on your computer. You can either work through from beginning to end or skip around to master the skills you need. If you have a specific goal you want to accomplish now, choose it from the following section.

SELECT YOUR GOALS

❖ I would like help installing WordPerfect 6.

Go to Appendix A, "Installing WordPerfect 6 for Windows."

❖ I'm new to WordPerfect and I want to learn how to create and print a letter.

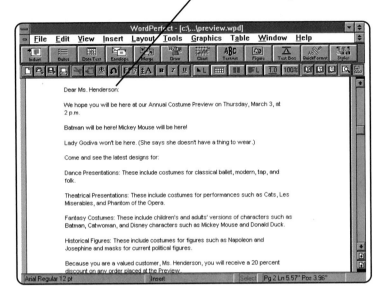

Turn to Part I, "Entering, Editing, and Printing Text," to learn how to set margins, change the font, and enter text. You'll also learn how to save, name, and print a document and use the spelling checker, grammar checker, and Thesaurus.

I want to know how to customize a document.

❖ Turn to Part II, "Formatting a Document," to learn how to customize text by changing the type style to bold, italics, or underlined. You will add a header and a page number, and set tabs. You will also learn how to center text and create special effects, such as a bulleted list and a shaded border.

❖ I want to set up a table.

Turn to Part IV, "Introducing Tables," to learn how to create a table, edit a table, format numbers, and write formulas.

❖ I want to know how to use WordPerfect's special Envelope button.

Turn to Chapter 11, "Printing an Envelope," to learn how to print a single envelope.

Chapter 16, "Printing Envelopes for a Mailing List," covers how to print merge envelopes.

❖ I want to learn how to create and print a personalized version of a form letter for a list of people.

In Chapter 12, you will learn how to create a mailing list. Chapter 13 teaches you how to edit a mailing list and Chapters 14 and 15 show you how to set up and print a personalized version of a form letter. Chapter 16 covers how to print envelopes for your mailing list. If you are switching to WordPerfect 6 from another word-processing program, such as Word 6 or WordStar, see Chapter 17 in Part III to learn how to convert a mailing list from another program.

❖ I want to learn how to do file management tasks.

Turn to Part V, "Special Features." You will learn how to print multiple files. You will also learn how to create a new directory and move files to it.

Program Manager

Part I Entering, Editing, and Printing Text

Changing Margins and Fonts, and Entering Text

If you've never used WordPerfect for Windows, you are in for a treat. If you are upgrading to version 6, you will love the exciting new features. In this chapter you will do the following:

❖ Open a WordPerfect document
❖ Set margins
❖ Change the font for the current document
❖ Change the font for all future documents
❖ Enter text
❖ Use special fonts to insert symbols into the text

OPENING WORDPERFECT FOR THE FIRST TIME

1. Type win at the c:\> (C prompt) on your screen to open, or boot up, Windows. You will probably have different group icons at the bottom of your screen than you see in this example.

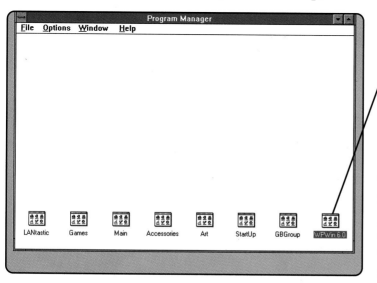

2. Click twice quickly on the **WPWin 6.0** group icon or the group icon that contains WordPerfect. It will open up to a group window that contains a number of icons. It's okay if your group window is in a different shape or position than the one you see in the next example.

3. **Click twice** on the WPWin 6.0 application icon. You will see an hourglass, then the copyright information for WordPerfect. Then, after a brief time, you will see the opening WordPerfect screen shown below.

Notice the title bar says "WordPerfect - [Document1-unmodified]." This will change when you name the document in Chapter 2, "Naming and Saving a Document."

The menu bar is under the title bar.

The power bar contains icons, or pictures, that represent common tasks like printing a file, checking your spelling, and changing the line spacing in your document. You will learn how to use these features later in this book.

In the next section you will learn to display the button bar, another powerful feature of WordPerfect.

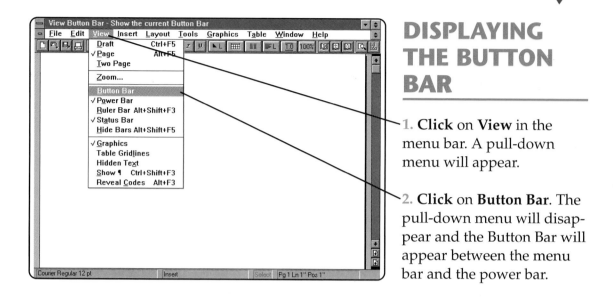

DISPLAYING THE BUTTON BAR

1. Click on **View** in the menu bar. A pull-down menu will appear.

2. Click on **Button Bar**. The pull-down menu will disappear and the Button Bar will appear between the menu bar and the power bar.

SETTING MARGINS

The standard (default) margins in WordPerfect are preset at 1 inch for the top, bottom, left, and right margins. You can change any or all of these settings as many times as you want within a document. Each time you make a change, the new margin applies from then on until you change it again. In this example you will change the top margin.

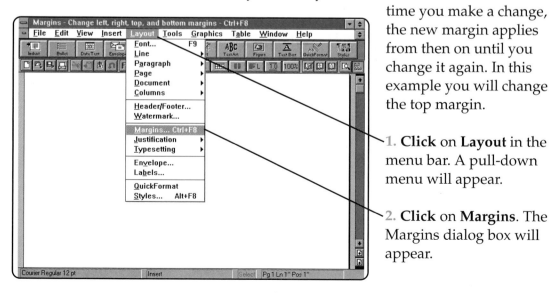

1. Click on **Layout** in the menu bar. A pull-down menu will appear.

2. Click on **Margins**. The Margins dialog box will appear.

3. **Click twice** on the ▼ to the right of the Top Margin box. The 1″ will change to 0.800″. You are making the top margin smaller than standard to give yourself the extra room to create the letterhead in the example in this chapter. (If you are going to print on stationery that already has a letterhead, the top margin for a short-to-medium-length letter should be about 2.5 inches.)

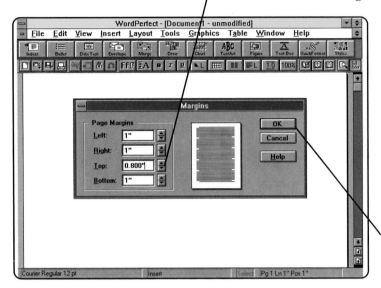

4. **Click** on **OK**. The Margin dialog box will disappear.

CHANGING THE FONT

When you change the font in a document on your screen, it affects only that document. However, you can change the default, or initial, font so that all future documents are affected.

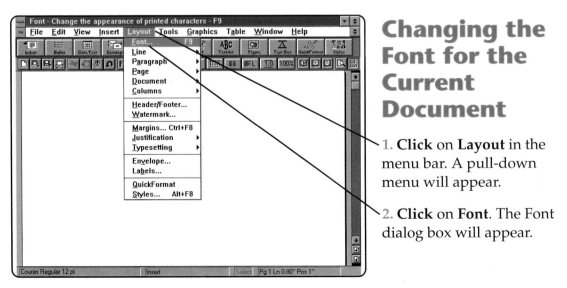

Changing the Font for the Current Document

1. **Click** on **Layout** in the menu bar. A pull-down menu will appear.

2. **Click** on **Font**. The Font dialog box will appear.

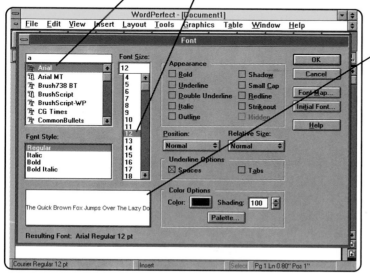

The font that is highlighted when this dialog box first opens is determined by the printer driver you selected during installation. In this example Courier is highlighted. You may have another font, such as Times New Roman, highlighted.

3. **Type** the letter **a**. This will move the highlight bar in the Font Face box up to the first beginning with the letter a.

4. **Click** on **Arial** if it is not already highlighted. (Arial may not be the first font on your list.)

Notice that 12 is already in the Font Size box. Because business correspondence is usually typed in a 10- or 12-point type, leave the font size at 12.

Notice the sample of the selected font in the Resulting Font box. Use the ↓ key on your keyboard to move through the list of fonts and watch the sample font change. However, if you want your screen to look like the examples in the book, make sure you go back to Arial.

Continue on to the next section to change the font for page numbers, headers, footers, and notes.

CHANGING THE FONT FOR PAGE NUMBERS, HEADERS, FOOTERS, AND NOTES

The font for page numbers, headers, footers, and notes is controlled by a different dialog box than the Font dialog box, which controls the text in the letter. In this example you will change this font to Arial to match the font for the body of the document.

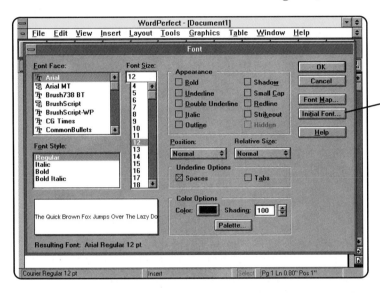

1. **Click** on **Initial Font** in the Font dialog box. The Document Initial Font dialog box will appear. (If you have not been following along with this chapter, go back to the previous section, "Changing the Font," to open the Font dialog box.)

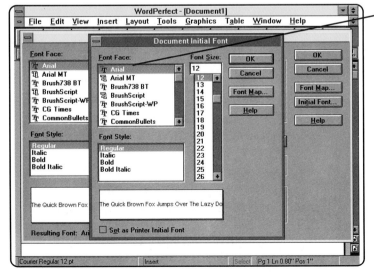

2. **Type** the letter **a** to move the highlight bar to the top of the Font Face list if the highlight bar is not already there.

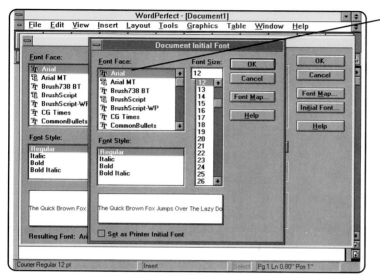

3. **Click** on **Arial** if it is not already highlighted.

4. **Leave** the **Font Size** at **12**.

You can change the font for all future documents to Arial in this dialog box. So instead of clicking on OK to close the dialog box, go on to the following section to change the Initial Font.

Changing the Font for Future Documents

If you have not been following along with this chapter, go back and follow the steps under "Changing the Font" to open the Font dialog box and then the Document Initial Font dialog box.

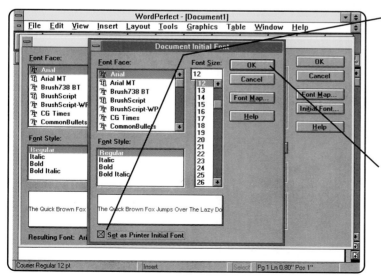

1. **Click** on **Set as Printer Initial Font** to insert an ✕ in the box. This tells WordPerfect to change the font that will appear in all future documents to Arial 12 point type.

2. **Click** on **OK**. The Document Initial Font dialog box will disappear. The Font dialog box will still be on your screen.

3. **Click** on **OK** to close the Font dialog box.

ENTERING TEXT

You are now ready to type a letter. In the following examples you will type a letter from the Coburn Costume Company inviting a customer to the Annual Costume Preview.

Creating the Letterhead

The insertion point will be flashing at the beginning of the document. This means you can start typing and the text will begin at this point. The first thing you will type is the company name and return address.

1. **Press** the **Caps Lock key** to turn on the capital letters function so that the text you type will appear as capital letters.

2. **Type COBURN COSTUME COMPANY** and **press Enter**. The insertion point will move to line 2.

3. **Press Caps Lock** again to turn off the capital letters function.

4. Type "All the world's a stage" and **press Enter**.

5. Type 2211 Garden Drive and **press Enter**.

6. Type San Diego, CA 92024. (Press the Spacebar twice after CA.) **Press Enter**.

7. Type (619) 555-7777.

8. Press Enter six times.

Entering the Date, Address, and Salutation

1. Place (do not click) the mouse pointer **on the Date Text button** in the button bar.

Notice that in the title bar the function of this button is described. As you slide your mouse pointer across the button bar and power bar or other elements of the screen their function will also be described in the title bar.

2. **Click** on the **Date Text button**.

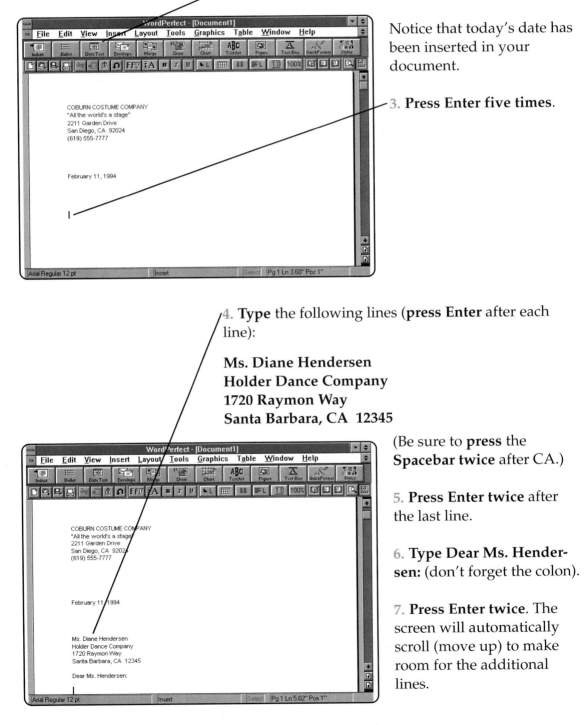

Notice that today's date has been inserted in your document.

3. **Press Enter five times**.

4. **Type** the following lines (**press Enter** after each line):

Ms. Diane Hendersen
Holder Dance Company
1720 Raymon Way
Santa Barbara, CA 12345

(Be sure to **press** the **Spacebar twice** after CA.)

5. **Press Enter twice** after the last line.

6. **Type Dear Ms. Hendersen:** (don't forget the colon).

7. **Press Enter twice**. The screen will automatically scroll (move up) to make room for the additional lines.

Entering the Body of the Letter

You are now ready to enter the body of the letter. Like all word-processing programs, you can type without worrying about your right margin. WordPerfect will wrap the text around to the next line automatically.

There is another way in which word processing is different from typing. On the typewriter you press the spacebar twice after a period at the end of a sentence. In word processing you press the spacebar only once after the period at the end of a sentence.

1. **Type** the text below. It contains errors (shown in red) that you will correct later, so include them if you want to follow along with these procedures. If you make an unintentional typing error, press the Backspace key and type the correct letters.

We hope you will be her at our Annual Costume Preview on Thursday, March 3, at 2 p.m. (Remember to press Enter twice at the end of this sentence to begin a new paragraph.)

Note: As you type the body of the letter, you may notice minor differences in which words move to the next line. It's perfectly alright to have slight differences. Just be aware that the differences are because your printer and driver are probably different from the ones we use and not because of any mistake on your part. (We are using a LaserJet II.)

General Status - Display info for columns, tables, macros, merge, paragraph styles, etc.

File   Edit   View   Insert   Layout   Tools   Graphics   Table   Window   Help

Indent   Bullet   Date Text   Envelope   Merge   Draw   Chart   TextArt   Figure   Text Box   QuickFormat   Styles

COBURN COSTUME COMPANY
"All the world's a stage"
2211 Garden Drive
San Diego, CA 92024
(619) 555-7777

February 11, 1994

Ms. Diane Hendersen
Holder Dance Company
1720 Raymon Way
Santa Barbara, CA 12345

Dear Ms. Hendersen:

We hope you will be her at our Annual Costume Preview on Thursday, March 3, at 2 p.m.

Arial Regular 12 pt   Insert   Select   Pg 1 Ln 5.59" Pos 1"

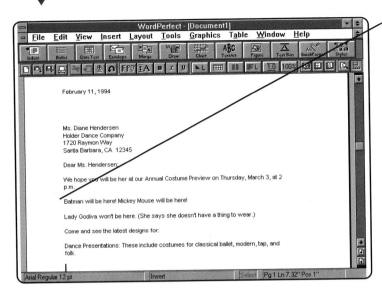

Batman will be here! Mickey Mouse will be here!

Lady Godiva won't be here. (She says she doesn't have a thing to wear.)

Come and see the latest designs for:

Dance Presentations: These include costumes for classical ballet, modern, tap, and folk. (Press Enter twice to begin the next paragraph.)

Theatrical Presentations: These include costumes for performances such as Cats, Les Miserables, and Phantom of the Opera.

Fantasy Costumes: These include childrens and adults' versions of characters such as Batman, Catwoman, and Disney characters such as Mickey Mouse. (Remember to **press Enter twice** to start the next paragraph.)

Historical Figures: These include costumes for figures such as Napoleon and Josephine and masks for current political figures.

Because you are a valued customer, Ms. Hendersen, you will recieve a 20 percent discount on any order placed at the Preview.

Please return a copy of the reply form below by Wednesday, February 23.

2. **Press Enter twice** after the last line.

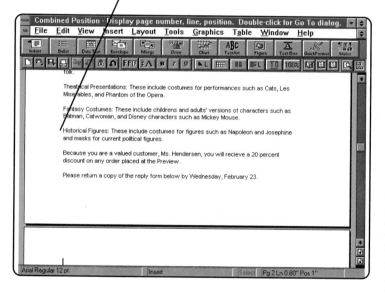

Notice that you have moved to a new page on the screen. This is the *automatic page break*. You will learn how to change the location of the page break in Chapter 6, "Editing a Document."

The exact location of the automatic page break depends on the margins you set and the size of the font you use. It also depends on the printer and printer driver you select.

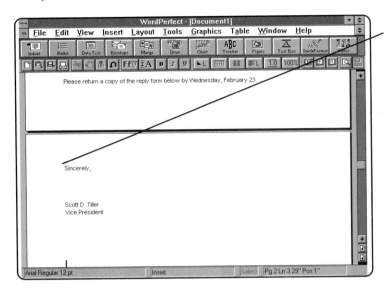

3. Type Sincerely,

4. Press Enter five times.

5. Type Scott D. Tiller and **press Enter.**

6. Type Vice President.

7. Press Enter seven times. Your screen will look like this example.

INSERTING SYMBOLS AND FINISHING THE LETTER

WordPerfect 6 for Windows comes with a variety of character sets that range from symbols to foreign language alphabets. In this section, you will insert two different symbols into the text.

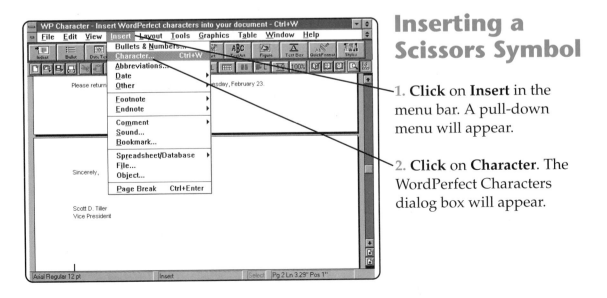

Inserting a Scissors Symbol

1. Click on **Insert** in the menu bar. A pull-down menu will appear.

2. Click on **Character**. The WordPerfect Characters dialog box will appear.

Notice Iconic Symbols is selected.

3. Click three times on the ⬇ on the scroll bar in the dialog box so that you can see the scissors.

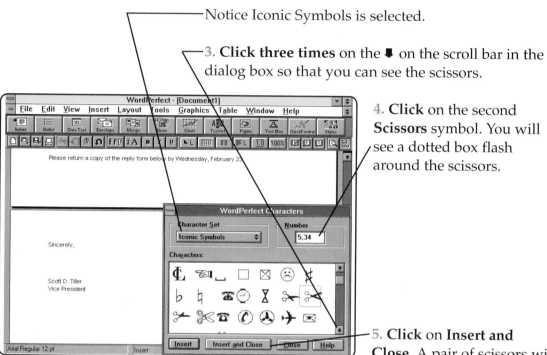

4. Click on the second **Scissors** symbol. You will see a dotted box flash around the scissors.

5. Click on **Insert and Close**. A pair of scissors will be inserted into your text.

6. Press and hold the **hyphen key** on your keyboard to type a dotted line across the page. If you go too far and the hyphens start showing on the second line, simply press the Backspace key until the cursor is at the end of the first line of hyphens.

7 Press the **Enter key twice** to move the cursor down two lines after the hyphens.

Inserting Box Symbols

1. **Repeat steps 1 and 2** in the previous section to open the WordPerfect Characters dialog box.

2. **Click once** on the ⬇ on the scroll bar so that you can see the square.

3. **Click** on the **square** symbol in the third line.

4. **Click** on **Insert and Close**. The square symbol will be inserted into the letter.

5. **Press** the **Spacebar**. Then **type** the sentence **I will be attending**. Then **press Enter twice**.

6. **Repeat steps 1 through 4** to insert another square into the text.

7. **Type** the sentence **I will be sending a representative from my company**. Then **press Enter twice**.

8. **Repeat steps 1 through 4** to insert the square into the text a third time.

9. Type the following sentences: **I will not be able to attend. Please send me your latest catalog**. Then **press Enter twice**.

```
                WordPerfect - [Document1]
 File  Edit  View  Insert  Layout  Tools  Graphics  Table  Window  Help

[toolbar icons: Indent  Bullet  Date Text  Envelope  Merge  Draw  Chart  TextArt  Figure  Text Box  QuickFormat  Styles]
[toolbar icons row: B  I  U  ...  100% ...]


        Sincerely,



        Scott D. Tiller
        Vice President




        ><----------------------------------------------------------------

        □ I will be attending.

        □ I will be sending a representative from my company.

        □ I will not be able to attend. Please send my your latest catalog.

        Please mail to the address at the top of the first page, or FAX us your reply at (619)
        555-1202.

Arial Regular 12 pt              Insert              Select   Pg 2 Ln 5.06" Pos 1.75"
```

10. Type the sentence **Please mail to the address at the top of the first page, or FAX us your reply at (619) 555-1202.**

Congratulations! You just created a letter in WordPerfect. In Chapter 2, you will name the letter and save it.

Naming and Saving a Document

Saving a document, or file, in WordPerfect is as easy as clicking your mouse. WordPerfect is setup to save files to the WPDOCS directory, which is a sub-directory of WPWIN60. In this chapter you will do the following:

❖ Name and save a document

NAMING AND SAVING A FILE

In this section you will name the letter you typed in Chapter 1 and save it to the WPDOCS directory.

1. **Click** on the **Save** button in the power bar. Because you have not named the file, the Save As dialog box will appear.

Notice that this is a magnified view of the upper-left corner of your screen. You will see both regular views and magnified views in this book.

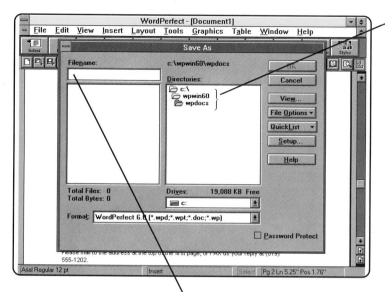

Notice the open folders beside c:\, wpwin60, and wpdocs. These tell you that you are currently working in wpdocs, which is a subdirectory of wpwin60. Both the wpwin60 and the wpdocs subdirectory are on the C drive.

Directories are organized in outline order like an outline for a term paper. The C drive (c:\) is a first-level category. Then wpwin60 is a second-level category under that. Then wpdocs is a subdirectory, or third-level category, under wpwin60.

Because the cursor is already flashing in the Filename box and the correct folders are open, you can simply go to step 2 and type a name for your file. Filenames can have no more than eight characters with no spaces.

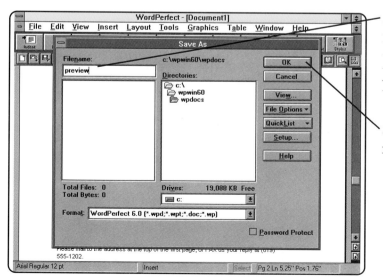

2. **Type preview**. WordPerfect will automatically add the .wpd extension (for WordPerfect document) when it saves the file.

3. **Click** on **OK**. Your file is now saved.

Notice that the document is now named preview.wpd-unmodified.

As you work on a file, use the Save button often. After you have named a file, clicking on the Save button will not bring up the Save As dialog box. It will simply save any changes you have made to your file.

Printing a Document

In WordPerfect 6 for Windows, you can print the whole document, the current page, or selected pages. You can click on the Print button in the power bar or you can use the File pull-down menu. Both methods will bring up the Print dialog box. In this chapter you will do the following:

❖ Print all or part of a document using the Print button

❖ Use the File pull-down menu to print all or part of a document

PRINTING A DOCUMENT WITH THE PRINT BUTTON

In this section you will use the Print button in the power bar to print a document. If you do not have a file open, open one now. Also, make sure your printer is turned on or you will get an error message when you try to print.

Print - Print a document - F5

File Edit View Insert Layout Tools

Indent Bullet Date Text Envelope Merge Draw

FFF A B I

Sincerely,

Scott D. Tiller

1. **Click** on the **Print button** in the power bar. The Print dialog box will appear.

From the Print dialog box you can print the current page, a range of pages, or the entire document. The following examples will show you how.

Printing the Current Page

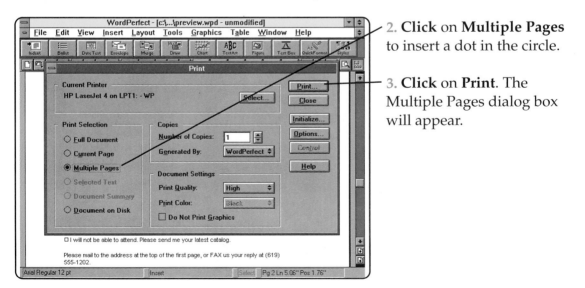

1. Click on **Current Page** to insert a dot in the circle. This instructs WordPerfect to print only the page where your cursor is located.

2. Click on **Print**. After a brief pause the current page will print.

Printing Selected Pages

1. Click on the **Print button** in the power bar to open the Print dialog box.

2. Click on **Multiple Pages** to insert a dot in the circle.

3. Click on **Print**. The Multiple Pages dialog box will appear.

Notice "all" is highlighted in the Page(s) box.

4. **Type 3,5,9-15**. It will replace the highlighted "all". This specifies that pages 3, 5, and 9 through 15 are to be printed. Since this document isn't that long, cancel out of this dialog box. If the document were that long, you would simply click on Print.

5. **Click** on **Cancel**. The Print dialog box will reappear.

Printing the Entire Document

1. **Click** on **Full Document** to insert a dot in the circle.

2. **Click** on **Print**. You will see a message box saying "Preparing document for printing." Then the entire document will print.

PRINTING A DOCUMENT WITH THE FILE PULL-DOWN MENU

Using the File pull-down menu will also bring up the Print dialog box.

1. Click on **File** in the menu bar. A pull-down menu will appear.

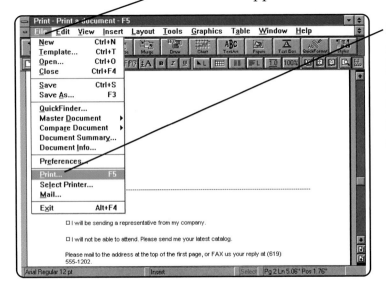

2. Click on **Print**. The Print dialog box will appear. Refer to the steps shown earlier in the chapter to print the current page, selected pages, or the entire document.

Closing a File and Opening a Saved File

Because WordPerfect 6 for Windows is a Windows-based program, it uses standard Windows commands to open and close files. As in all Windows programs, there are several ways to open and close files. In this chapter you will do the following:

❖ Close a file

❖ Close WordPerfect for Windows

❖ Learn two ways to open a saved file

CLOSING A FILE

In this section you will close the preview.wpd file you created in Chapter 1. Because WordPerfect will prompt you to save if you have made any changes since your last save, there is no need to worry about losing changes to your file.

1. **Click** on **File** in the menu bar. A pull-down menu will appear.

2. **Click** on **Close**.

If you have not made any changes to preview.wpd since you saved in Chapter 2, WordPerfect will simply close the file and a blank WordPerfect screen will appear.

Close - Close the current document window - Ctrl+F4

| File | Edit | View | Insert | Layout | Tools | Graphics | Table | Window | Help |

New   Ctrl+N
Template... Ctrl+T
Open...   Ctrl+O
Close   Ctrl+F4

Save   Ctrl+S
Save As...   F3

QuickFinder...
Master Document
Compare Document
Document Summary...
Document Info...

Preferences...

Print...   F5
Select Printer...
Mail...

Exit   Alt+F4

☐ I will be sending a representative from my company.

☐ I will not be able to attend. Please send me your latest catalog.

Please mail to the address at the top of the first page, or FAX us your reply at (619) 555-1202.

Arial Regular 12 pt | Insert | Select | Pg 2 Ln 5.06" Pos 1.76"

Your screen will look like the example to the left.

Closing After Changes

Note: If you have been following along with the previous chapters, you won't see the screen in the following example because you saved your document before you closed it.

If, however, you have made changes since the last time you saved, you will see the following screen when you try to close the file.

a. Click on **Yes** to save the changes to the file.

or

b. Click on **No** to close without saving.

or

c. Click on **Cancel** if you change your mind or need to do something else first such as save your latest changes to a different file.

CLOSING WORDPERFECT FOR WINDOWS

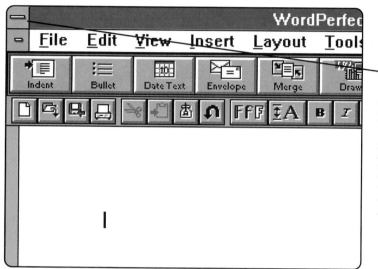

In this section you will close the WordPerfect program.

1. **Click twice** on the **Control menu box** (⊟) on the left of the WordPerfect title bar. After a pause WordPerfect will close and you will be back at Program Manager with the group that contains the WordPerfect icon.

BOOTING UP WORDPERFECT

"Boot up" is computer talk for start.

1. **Click twice** on the **WPWin 6.0** icon in whatever group it happens to be.

After a pause, WordPerfect will appear on your screen with a blank Document1 file.

OPENING A SAVED FILE

There are several ways to open a saved file. In Method #1, you will use the file pull-down menu.

Method #1

1. **Click** on **File** in the menu bar. A pull-down menu will appear.

At the bottom of the File pull-down menu you will see up to four files listed depending on whether you have a new WordPerfect program or others have used WordPerfect before you.

2. **Click** on **preview.wpd** in the file list. The file will appear on your screen.

Method #2

Method #2 uses the Open button in the power bar. To try this method, you will have to close the preview.wpd file.

1. **Click twice** on the **Control menu box** (⊟) to the left of the menu bar to close the file. (Be careful not to click on the Control menu box in the WordPerfect title bar. That will close the entire program.)

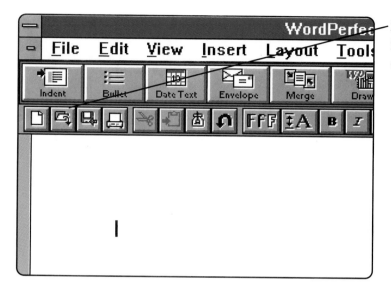

2. **Click** on the **Open button** in the power bar. The Open dialog box will appear.

Notice that the wpdocs directory appears in the directories list box.

3. **Click twice** on **preview.wpd** in the File-name list box. The file will appear on your screen. If others have used WordPerfect, you may have other files listed in this box. (You can also click once on preview.wpd to highlight it, then click on OK.)

In the next chapter you will learn how to use the Grammar and Spelling Checkers and the Thesaurus that comes with WordPerfect.

Using the Grammar Checker, Spelling Checker, and Thesaurus

WordPerfect has two handy utilities that will check your grammar and spelling and make suggestions for changes. It also contains a Thesaurus that will offer a list of synonyms and antonyms. Now, if it would only go out for coffee . . .

In this chapter you will do the following:

❖ Use Grammatik, WordPerfect's grammar checker
❖ Set the Spelling Checker to check from the cursor to the end of the document
❖ Use the Thesaurus

CHECKING GRAMMAR

You can check the grammar in an entire document, but in this example you will check the grammar in only one sentence of the preview.wpd document.

1. Press and hold the **Ctrl key** then **press** the **Home key** (Ctrl + Home). This will move the cursor to the beginning of the file if you are not already there.

2. Click repeatedly on the ⬇ on the scroll bar to bring the first two paragraphs into view.

```
WordPerfect - [c:\...\preview.wpd - unmodified]
File   Edit   View   Insert   Layout   Tools   Graphics   Table   Window   Help


COBURN COSTUME COMPANY
"All the world's a stage"
2211 Garden Drive
San Diego, CA  92024
(619) 555-7777



February 11, 1994



Ms. Diane Hendersen
Holder Dance Company
1720 Raymon Way
Santa Barbara, CA  12345

Dear Ms. Hendersen:

Arial Regular 12 pt          Insert          Select   Pg 1 Ln 0.80" Pos 1"
```

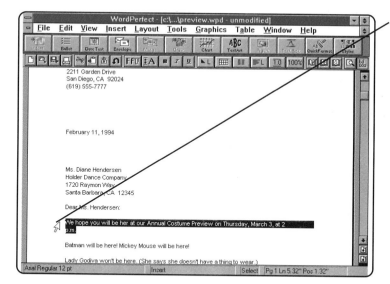

3. Click in the margin to the left of the first sentence. The mouse pointer will be in the shape of an arrow. This will highlight the entire paragraph.

4. Click on **Tools** in the menu bar. A pull-down menu will appear.

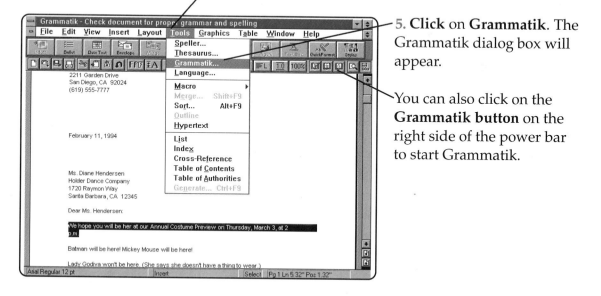

5. Click on **Grammatik**. The Grammatik dialog box will appear.

You can also click on the **Grammatik button** on the right side of the power bar to start Grammatik.

Moving the Grammatik Dialog Box

If the Grammatik dialog box covers the highlighted sentence, as it does in this example, you can move the dialog box.

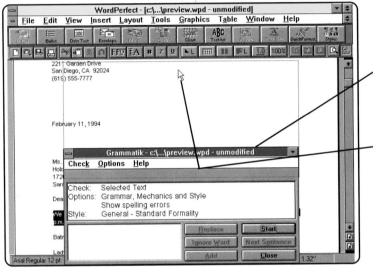

1. **Place** the **mouse arrow** on top of the Grammatik title bar.

2. **Press and hold** the mouse button and **drag** the dialog box up to the top of the letter. The dialog box will stay where it is and you will see an outline being dragged.

3. **Release** the mouse button. The dialog box will appear in place of the outline.

Starting Grammatik

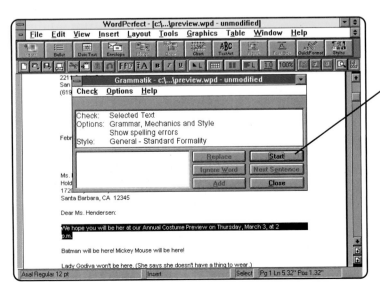

1. **Click** on **Start**. The first error that Grammatik finds will be highlighted in the text and will appear in the Grammatik dialog box.

Grammatik has identified the 2 in 2 p.m. as an error and says that 2 should be written as a word. This is an example of a rule that does not apply to the highlighted sentence. Because 2 p.m. indicates time, 2 is correctly written as a number. Therefore, skip this suggested change.

2. Click on **Skip**. Grammatik will identify the next error.

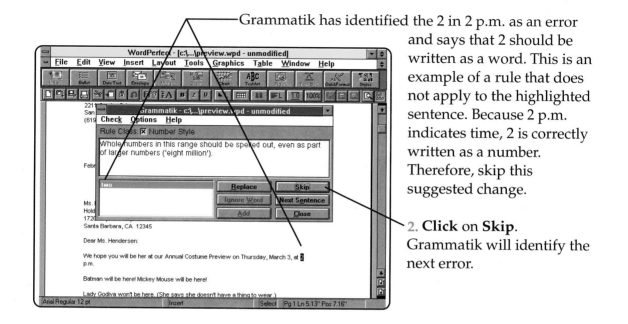

Grammatik has identified "her" as an error, but for the wrong reason. This is another example of why computers are not ready to rule the world. In this example the suggested replacement is not appropriate so you will have to edit the word directly in the document.

3. Click to the **right of "her"** in the letter.

4. Type the letter **e** to change the word to here.

5. Click on **Resume**. Grammatik will highlight the next error.

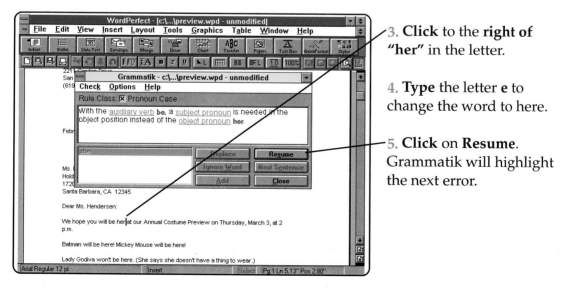

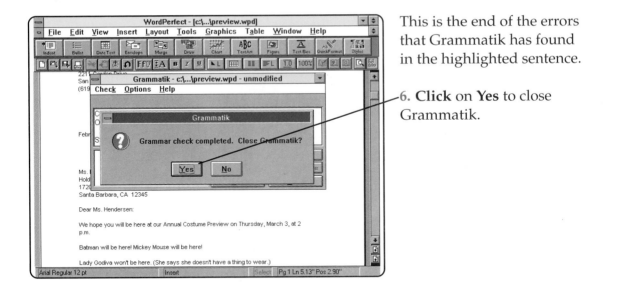

This is the end of the errors that Grammatik has found in the highlighted sentence.

6. **Click** on **Yes** to close Grammatik.

CHECKING SPELLING

WordPerfect is set up to check spelling from the beginning of a document. In this example, however, you will tell WordPerfect to begin checking from the cursor position.

1. **Click** to the **left of "We"** in the first sentence to place your cursor.

2. **Click** on the **Spelling Checker button** on the right of the power bar. The Speller dialog box will appear. (You can also click on Tools in the menu bar, then click on Speller.)

Checking From the Cursor

1. Click on **Check** in the spelling Checker menu bar. A pull-down menu will appear.

2. Click on **To End of Document**. This tell WordPerfect to begin the spelling check at the cursor and to continue to the end of the document.

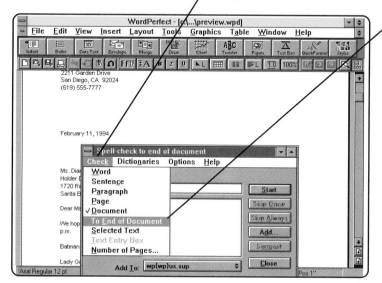

3. Click and hold on the **title bar** of the Speller dialog box and **drag** it up to the top of the document. You will see an outline of the dialog box as you drag. This will move the dialog box out of the way.

4. Click on **Start** after you have repositioned the dialog box.

The Spell Checker has identified Godiva as a misspelled or unknown word.

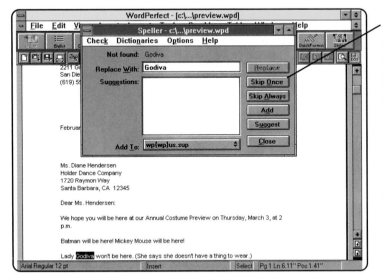

5. **Click** on **Skip Once**. This will skip the word once but the Spell Checker will highlight the word the next time it appears in the document.

6. **Click** on **Skip Once** when Speller identifies each of the following words as misspelled:

> Les
> Miserables

Correcting a Word in the Speller Dialog Box

The Spell Checker has identified childrens as a misspelled word but the suggestions do not include a plural possessive form. However, you can correct the word in the dialog box.

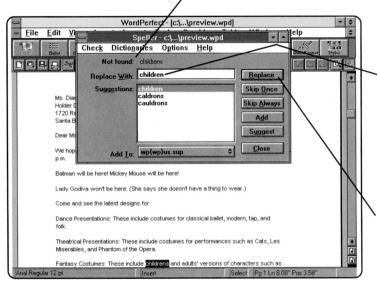

1. **Click** at the **end of children** in the Replace With box.

2. **Type 's** (an apostrophe and the letter s) to change the word to children's.

3. **Click** on **Replace**. The Spell Checker will next identify Catwoman as a misspelled word.

Adding a Word to the Dictionary

WordPerfect uses a standard dictionary to check words. If you use a non-standard word frequently (such as a proper name), you can add it to a supplemental dictionary. WordPerfect gives you two options for adding to the dictionary. You can add to a dictionary for the individual document or you can add the word to a dictionary that applies to all documents. In this example you will add Catwoman to the Document Dictionary.

1. **Click and hold** on **wp{wp}us.sup** in the Add To box. A pop-up list will appear. (Make sure you hold the mouse button or the list will disappear.)

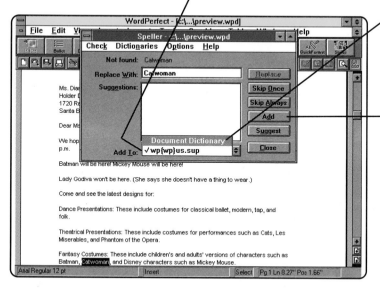

2. **Drag** the highlight bar up to **Document Dictionary** and then release the mouse button.

3. **Click** on **Add**. Catwoman is now added to the Document Dictionary.

If you had wanted to add Catwoman to the supplemental dictionary for all documents, you would simply have clicked on Add because wp{wp}us.sup was already showing in the Add To box.

The Spell Checker will go on to highlight the next misspelled or unrecognized word.

Completing the Spelling Check

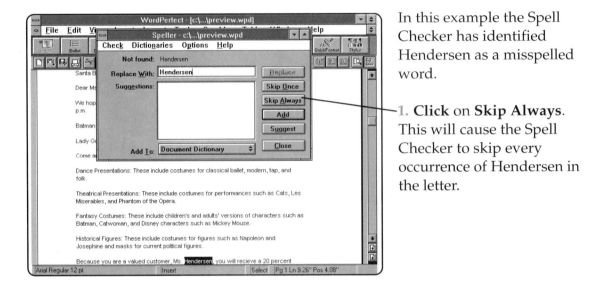

In this example the Spell Checker has identified Hendersen as a misspelled word.

1. Click on **Skip Always**. This will cause the Spell Checker to skip every occurrence of Hendersen in the letter.

In this example the Spell Checker has identified "recieve" as a misspelled word.

2. Because the correct word, receive, is highlighted in the suggestions list, **click** on **Replace**. The misspelled word will be replaced by the correct word.

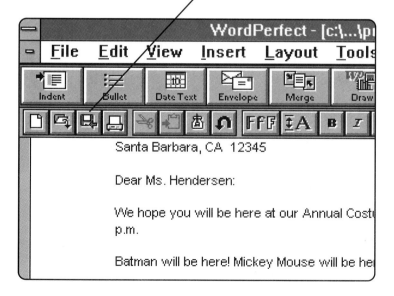

3. **Click** on **Yes** to close Speller.

Saving Your Work

1. **Click** on the **Save button** on the power bar to save the changes you have made.

USING THE THESAURUS

In this section you will use the Thesaurus to view words that can replace "latest." First, however, you will use the Find feature to locate "latest."

Using Find

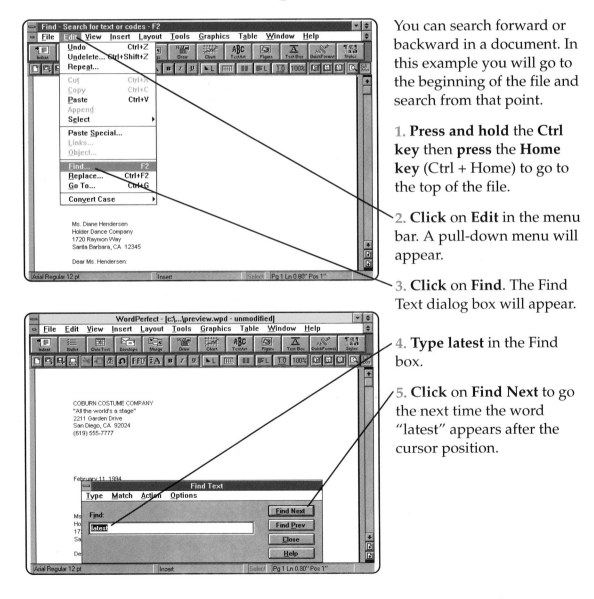

You can search forward or backward in a document. In this example you will go to the beginning of the file and search from that point.

1. **Press and hold** the **Ctrl key** then **press** the **Home key** (Ctrl + Home) to go to the top of the file.

2. **Click** on **Edit** in the menu bar. A pull-down menu will appear.

3. **Click** on **Find**. The Find Text dialog box will appear.

4. **Type latest** in the Find box.

5. **Click** on **Find Next** to go the next time the word "latest" appears after the cursor position.

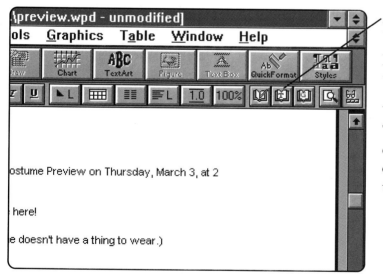

Notice that the first occurrence of latest is highlighted in the letter. Because this is the word you want to change, close the dialog box. (If you wanted another occurrence of latest, you would click on Find Next again until the one you wanted was highlighted.)

1. **Click** on **Close** to close the dialog box.

2. **Click** on the **Thesaurus button** on the right of the power bar. The Thesaurus dialog box will appear.

You can also bring up the Thesaurus dialog box by clicking on Tools then clicking on Thesaurus on the pull-down menu.

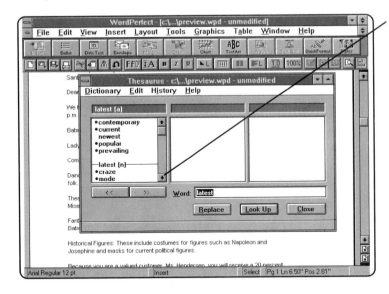

3. Click on the ⬇ on the scroll bar to scroll through the various choices. Notice the list begins with the synonyms for the adjective latest, latest [a].

Latest [n] lists synonyms for the noun latest.

Lastly, there are antonyms listed under latest [ant].

4. Click on ⬆ on the scroll bar to go back to the top of the list.

5. Click twice on **newest**. A second list will appear with synonyms and antonyms for newest.

If you click twice on a word in the second list, such as novels, a third list will appear with synonyms and antonyms for that word.

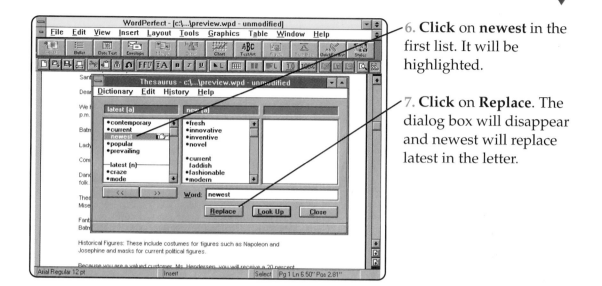

6. **Click** on **newest** in the first list. It will be highlighted.

7. **Click** on **Replace**. The dialog box will disappear and newest will replace latest in the letter.

8. **Click** on **File** in the menu bar. A pull-down menu will appear.

9. **Click** on **Save** to save your work. You can, of course, click on the Save button on the power bar instead of using the File pull-down menu. You can also press and hold the Ctrl key then type s (Ctrl + s) to save.

Editing a Document

WordPerfect 6 has a number of nifty editing features. Using the mouse and scroll bars makes moving through your document easy. Highlighting text allows you to delete, move, and copy with ease. You'll love the new drag-and-drop moving and copying features. You can even use an Edit Undo when you change your mind. In this chapter you will do the following:

❖ Add and delete letters and words and combine paragraphs

❖ Use the Edit Undo feature

❖ Use the Replace All command to correct an error that occurs in several places

❖ Move, copy, and paste text

❖ Insert and change the position of the page break

INSERTING TEXT

In this section you will add text to a paragraph. You will also learn to move around in your document.

Moving in a Document

1. **Press and hold** the **Ctrl key** and **press** the **Home key** (Ctrl + Home). This will place the cursor at the beginning of the file.

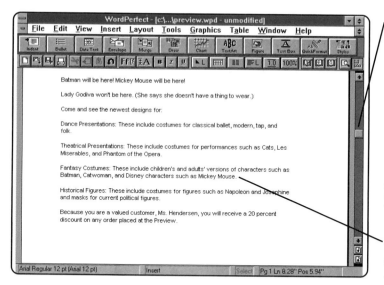

2. Place the **mouse arrow** on top of the Scroll button. On your screen it will be at the top of the scroll bar.

3. Click and hold as you **drag** the Scroll button **one third** of the way down the scroll bar. This will move you one third of the way through your document.

4. Click between "Mouse" and the period at the end of the "Fantasy Costumes" paragraph to place the cursor.

5. Press the **Spacebar** then **type** the phrase **and Donald Duck**. Notice the period moves as you type.

DELETING TEXT

In this section you will delete text from the same paragraph you edited above.

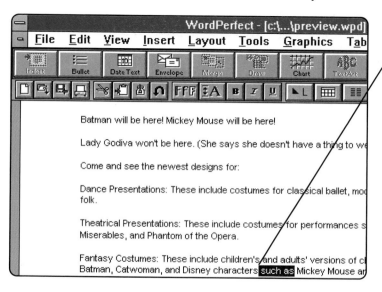

1. Click to the **right** of **Disney Characters** in the "Fantasy Costumes" paragraph to place the cursor.

2. Press and hold the mouse button and **drag** the cursor over **such as**. Be careful not to highlight the space after "as" or you will delete the space between the words.

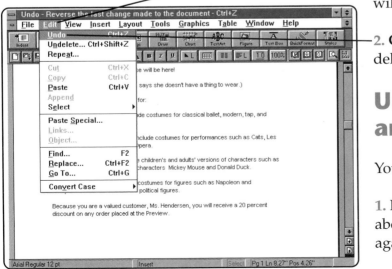

3. Press the **Delete key** on your keyboard. The highlighted text will be deleted. Notice that the rest of the sentence is automatically repositioned.

The sentence will look like the example to the left.

UNDOING AN EDIT

If you have been following along with this chapter, you just deleted the phrase "such as." What if that was a mistake and you didn't really mean to delete those words? WordPerfect has a wonderfully forgiving feature called Edit Undo. This feature will undo your very last action as long as you don't perform any other function before you use the Undo feature.

1. Click on **Edit** in the menu bar. A pull-down menu will appear.

2. Click on **Undo**. The deleted text will be restored.

Undoing an Undo

You can even undo an undo.

1. Repeat steps **1 and 2** above to delete the text once again.

COMBINING PARAGRAPHS

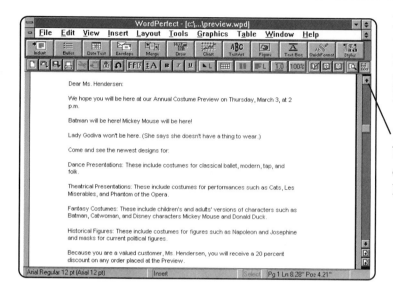

In this section you will put the Lady Godiva sentences into the preceding paragraph with Batman and Mickey Mouse.

1. Click on ⬆ on the scroll bar to scroll up so that you can see "Dear Ms. Hendersen."

2. Place the mouse pointer at the **beginning** of the **"Lady Godiva" sentence**. **Click** to place the cursor.

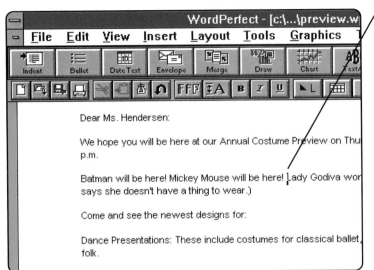

3. Press the **Backspace key twice.** Then **press** the **Spacebar.** This will bring the entire Lady Godiva paragraph up to the end of the Mickey Mouse sentence and put a space between the sentences.

OUTWITTING TEXT WRAP

Text wrap is the function within WordPerfect that automatically wraps long sentences to the next line. It does not always make the wrap in a place that makes sense.

It would, for example, make more sense if 2 and p.m. were together on one line instead of two different lines. If you move 2 to the second line with the Enter key, you will insert what is called a hard return. This means that this text will permanently stay as a separate line. It will not wrap back and forth between lines as you add and delete text. You can, however, move 2 to the next line by inserting what WordPerfect calls a *hard space.* A hard space is seen by the computer as an actual character rather than simply a space.

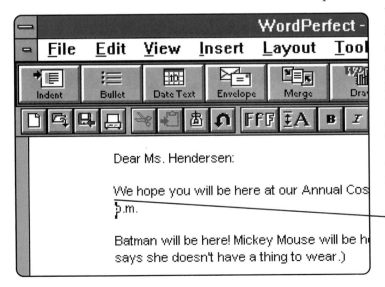

1. Click to the **left** of **p.m.** in the first sentence.

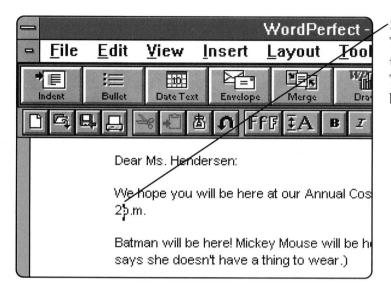

2. Press the **Backspace key.** This will bring 2 down to the second line with p.m. There will be no space between the words.

3. Click on **Layout**. A pull-down menu will appear.

4. Click on **Line**. Another menu will appear.

5. Click on **Other Codes**. The Other Codes dialog box will appear.

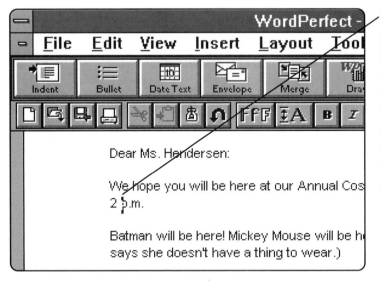

6. **Click** on **Hard Space [HSpace]** under the Other Codes category to insert a dot into the circle.

7. **Click** on **Insert**.

WordPerfect now considers 2 p.m. as one word. Because 2 p.m. is too long to fit on the first line, it will wrap to the second line. It will not be separated by any future text wrapping. A shortcut to inserting a hard space is to press and hold the Ctrl key and press the Spacebar (Ctrl + Spacebar).

Inserting a Hard Return

In this example, you will use a hard return to change the spacing in the very last line of the letter.

1. Press and hold the **Ctrl key** and **press** the **End key** (Ctrl + End). This will take you to the end of the document.

2. Click to the **left** of **"or"** in the last line of the letter.

3. Press Enter. This will move the cursor and the following text to the next line. These will now be two separate lines and will not wrap back and forth if you add or delete text.

USING THE REPLACE COMMAND

In this example you will replace "sen" at the end of "Hendersen" with "son." You can replace each "sen" individually or you can use the Replace command to find and replace each occurrence for you. You will start at the top of the file since the Replace command begins at the cursor and goes to the end of the file.

1. Press and hold the **Ctrl key** and **press** the **Home key** (Ctrl + Home) to go to the beginning of your file.

2. Click on **Edit** in the menu bar. A pull-down menu will appear.

3. Click on **Replace**. The Find and Replace Text dialog box will appear. The cursor will be in the Find text box.

4. Type Hendersen.

5. Click on the **Replace With box** and **type Henderson**.

6. Click on **Replace All**. WordPerfect will replace all occurrences of Hendersen with Henderson. You will be at the end of the file.

7. Click on **Close**.

DRAG-AND-DROP MOVING

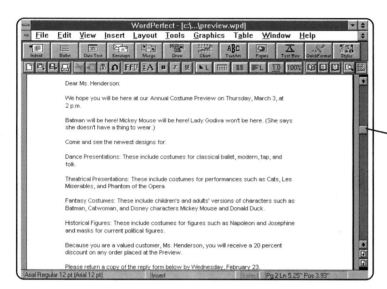

WordPerfect has a wonderful feature that lets you move text with your mouse. In this example you will move the first sentence.

1. Click and hold on the **scroll button** and **drag** it so that it is approximately **one-quarter** of the way from the top of the scroll bar. You should be able to see the first few paragraphs of the letter.

2. Place the **mouse arrow** in the **left margin** beside the first sentence.

3. Click once to highlight the entire sentence.

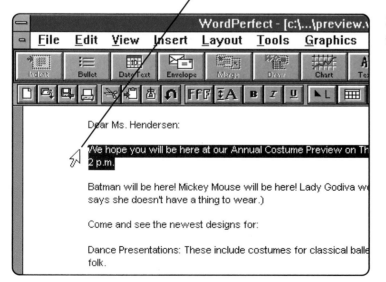

4. Place the mouse arrow **anywhere** on the highlighted text.

5. Press and hold the mouse button and **drag** the pointer down to the end of the next paragraph. You will see two squares being dragged by the arrow. A flashing bar will appear to the right of the parentheses.

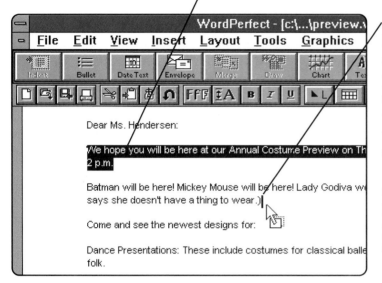

6. Release the mouse button. The highlighted paragraph will move to that spot.

7. Click to the **left** of **"We"** to move the highlighting and place the cursor.

8. Press Enter twice to move the "We hope" sentence to a new paragraph.

Notice there are now extra lines at the beginning of the letter.

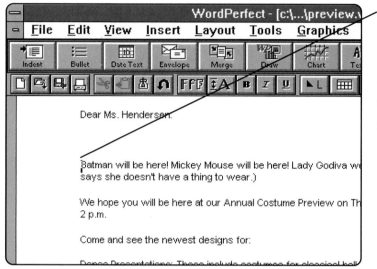

9. Click at the **beginning of the "Batman" sentence** to set the cursor in place.

10. Press Backspace twice. The text of the letter will be moved up two lines.

INSERTING A PAGE BREAK

WordPerfect does not necessarily insert an automatic page break in a place that makes sense within the context of the document. Fortunately, it's easy to change the position of the page break.

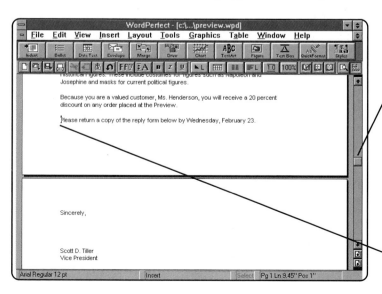

1. Click and hold on the **scroll button** and **drag** it half way down the scroll bar so it looks like the one in this example. You will be able to see the automatic page break.

2. Click to the **left** of the **"Please return" sentence.**

3. **Press and hold** the **Ctrl key** as you **press Enter**. A page break will be inserted into the text at the cursor.

The page break will appear at the position where you placed your cursor. The previous page break that was created automatically will disappear.

DELETING A PAGE BREAK

It's very easy to delete a page break that you have inserted into the document.

1. **Click** to the **left** of the **first line** below the page break if your cursor is not already there.

2. Press the **Backspace key**.

The text will be moved up one line and the inserted page break will disappear.

The automatic page break will reappear.

3. Press and hold the **Ctrl key** and **press Enter** to insert the page break at the "Please return sentence" again.

DRAG-AND-DROP COPYING

In this example you will copy the phrase "Annual Costume Preview on Thursday, March 3" from page 1 to page 2.

1. Press and hold the mouse pointer on the scroll button and **drag** the button up so you can see the first sentence.

2. Click to the **left** of **"Annual"** in the "We hope" sentence.

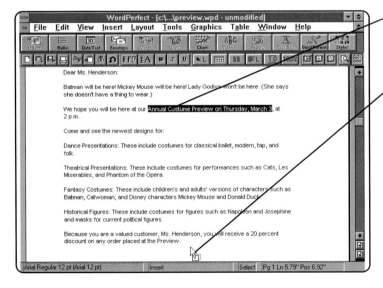

3. Press and hold the mouse button as you **drag** the highlight bar across to **March 3**. Do not highlight the comma after the 3.

4. Place the mouse **anywhere** on the highlighted text.

5. Press and hold the mouse button as you **drag** the cursor down the page. You will see the mouse arrow dragging two squares.

6. Continue to **press and hold** the mouse button as you **drag** the arrow down into the bottom of your screen. Suddenly your screen will start to scroll up. Continue to drag the arrow down until you can see the end of the letter.

7. Continue to **press and hold** the mouse button. **Place** the **cursor** and **mouse pointer** on the blank line **after the scissors**.

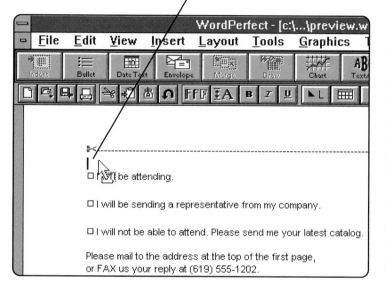

8. **Press and hold** the **Ctrl key**. Then release the mouse button. (Pressing the Ctrl key copies the highlighted text to the cursor spot instead of simply moving it as you did in drag-and-drop moving earlier in this chapter.)

If you forgot to press the Ctrl key, simply click on the Undo button in the power bar and try again.

Your screen will look like this example.

9. **Click** to the **left** of **on Thursday** to place the cursor.

10. **Press Enter** to move the cursor and the following text to the next line.

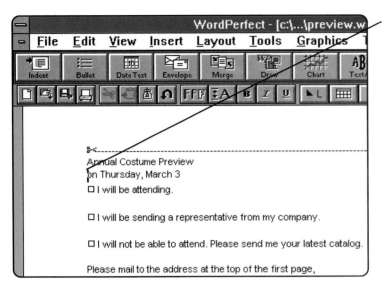

11. **Press** the **Delete key** on your keyboard **three times** to delete the word on and the space after it.

12. **Click** to the **right** of the number **3** to place the cursor.

13. **Press Enter twice** to insert two blank lines.

COPYING AND PASTING TEXT

In this three-part example you will use the Copy button, the Go To function, and the Paste button.

Copying the Text

1. **Press and hold** the **Ctrl key** and **press** the **Home key** (Ctrl + Home to go to the top of the file.

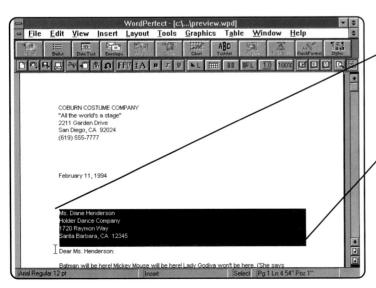

2. **Place** the mouse pointer immediately to the left of Ms. Diane Henderson. The pointer should be in the shape of an I-beam.

3. **Press and hold** the mouse button as you **drag** the pointer down to the blank line after the address. All four lines of text and the blank line will be highlighted.

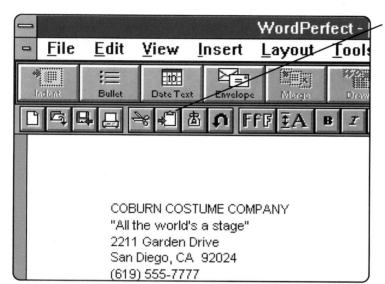

4. **Click** on the **Copy button** on the power bar. You won't see any change on your screen but the highlighted text has been copied to the clipboard, a temporary storage area in your computer's memory.

Using the Go To Command

Using the Go To command is a quick way to move around in multipage documents. In this example you will use it to go to the top of page 2.

1. **Click** on **Edit** in the menu bar. A pull-down menu will appear.

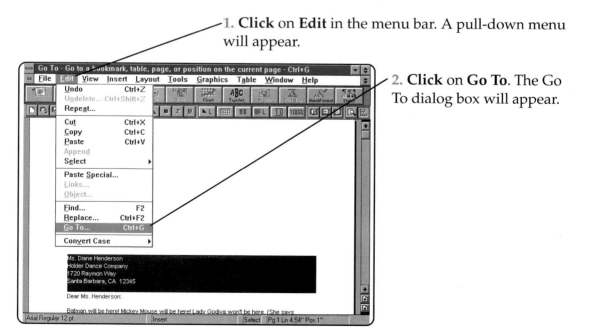

2. **Click** on **Go To**. The Go To dialog box will appear.

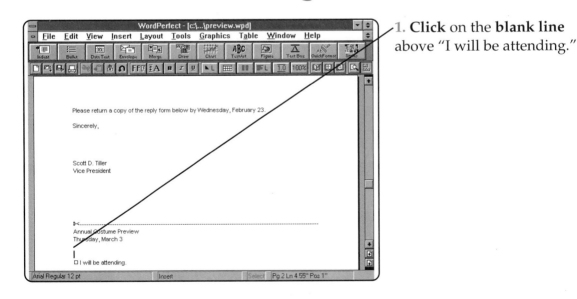

3. Type the number **2**. It will replace the highlighted number in the Page Number box.

4. Click on **OK**.

Your screen will show the top of page 2.

Pasting Text

1. Click on the **blank line** above "I will be attending."

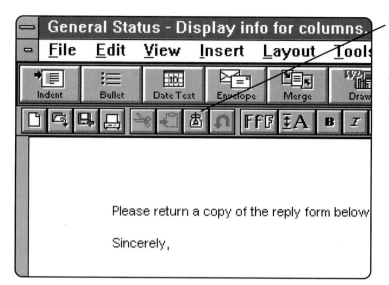

2. Click on the **Paste button** on the power bar. The text and blank line you copied will be pasted into the document at the cursor.

3. Click on the **Save button** on the power bar to save your work.

You will use this edited letter in Part II, "Formatting a Document."

Program Manager

Part II   Formatting a Document

Customizing Text

You will love how easy it is to customize the look of your text in WordPerfect 6. With just a few clicks of your mouse you can center text, change the type size, or make type bold, italics, or underlined. You can also create a bulleted list. In addition, you can add special borders around sections of your text then add shading inside the border to create an exciting visual effect. In this chapter you will do the following:

❖ Change type size

❖ Make text bold, italics, and underlined

❖ Center text

❖ Add a border around text and add shading inside the border

❖ Create a bulleted list

CHANGING TYPE SIZE

In this section you will increase the size of the type in the first line of the letter you created in Part I. If you don't already have preview.wpd open, open it now.

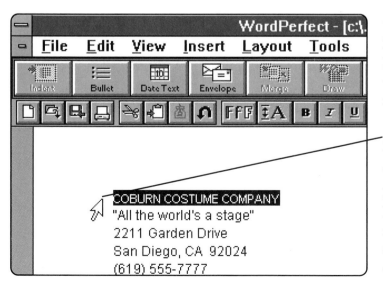

1. **Press and hold** the **Ctrl key** then **press** the **Home key** (Ctrl + Home) to go to the top of the file if you are not already there.

2. **Click** in the left margin **beside "COBURN COS-TUME COMPANY."** The line of text will be high-lighted. Make sure your mouse pointer is in the shape of an arrow when you click or this step won't work.

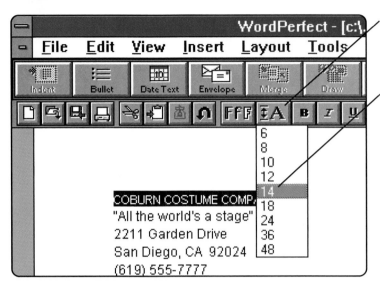

3. Click on the **Font Size button** in the power bar. A pull-down list will appear.

4. Click on **14**. The list will disappear and "COBURN COSTUME COMPANY" will change from a 12-point size to a 14-point size.

MAKING TEXT BOLD

In this section you will make the type, "COBURN COSTUME COMPANY," boldface.

1. Click in the **left margin** beside **"COBURN COSTUME COMPANY"** to highlight the text if it is not already highlighted.

2. Click on the **Bold button** in the power bar. the text will be made bold. The Bold button works like a toggle switch. Click it once, and the highlighted text is made bold. Click it again while the text is highlighted and the boldface is removed. Make sure to leave the text bold.

MAKING TEXT ITALIC

In this section you will italicize the line, "All the world's a stage."

1. Click in the **left margin** beside **"All the world's a stage"** to highlight it.

2. Click on the **Italics button** in the power bar. The text will be italicized. Like the Bold button, the Italics button also works like a toggle switch.

UNDERLINING TEXT

In this section you will underline text.

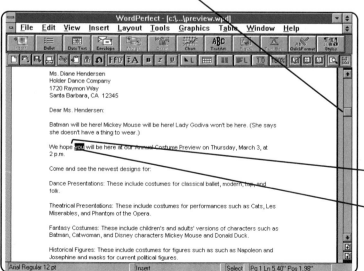

1. Click and drag the scroll button **one-quarter** of the way **down** the **scroll bar**. It will look like the one in this example. (If you scrolled too far up or down, click on the ⬆ or ⬇ on the scroll bar until you can see approximately the same text as in the example to the left.)

2. Click to the **left** of **"you."**

3. Press and hold the mouse button as you **drag** the highlight bar across **"you."**

Underline Font - Turn on underline font - Ctrl+U

File **Edit** **View** **Insert** **Layout** **Tools** **Graphics**

Indent Bullet Date Text Envelope Merge Draw Chart Text

Ms. Diane Hendersen
Holder Dance Company
1720 Raymon Way
Santa Barbara, CA 12345

Dear Ms. Hendersen:

Batman will be here! Mickey Mouse will be here! Lady Godiva wor
she doesn't have a thing to wear.)

We hope **you** will be here at our Annual Costume Preview on Thu
2 p.m.

Come and see the newest designs for:

4. **Click** on the **Underline button** in the power bar. The word "you" will be underlined.

If you accidentally underlined the space after "you," simply highlight the space and click on the Underline button to remove the underline

CHECKING TEXT STYLE

In this section you will learn a method to check if text has been modified from the default font and point size.

1. **Press and hold** the **Ctrl key** then **press** the **Home key** (Ctrl + Home) to go to the top of the file.

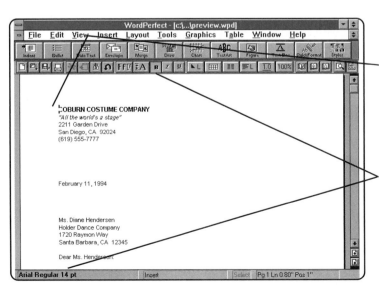

WordPerfect - [c:\...\preview.wpd]

File Edit View Insert Layout Tools Graphics Table Window Help

Indent Bullet Date Text Envelope Merge Draw Chart TextArt Figure QuickFormat Styles

COBURN COSTUME COMPANY
"All the world's a stage"
2211 Garden Drive
San Diego, CA 92024
(619) 555-7777

February 11, 1994

Ms. Diane Hendersen
Holder Dance Company
1720 Raymon Way
Santa Barbara, CA 12345

Dear Ms. Hendersen:

Arial Regular 14 pt   Insert   Select Pg 1 Ln 0.80" Pos 1"

2. **Click** to the **left** of **COBURN** so the cursor is flashing at the beginning of the first line of text as shown.

Notice that the font, bolding, and point size of 14 is indicated in the status line. Notice also that the Bold button in the power bar appears pressed in.

3. Click to the **left** of *"All the world's a stage"* so the cursor is flashing at the beginning of the line of text as shown.

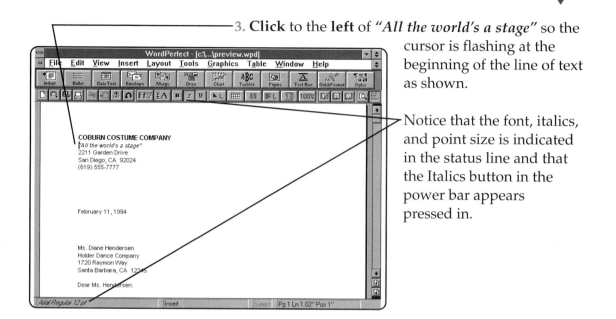

Notice that the font, italics, and point size is indicated in the status line and that the Italics button in the power bar appears pressed in.

4. Click and drag the **scroll button one-quarter** of the way down the scroll bar so that you can see the word "you" that you underlined earlier.

5. Click to the **left** of **"you."**

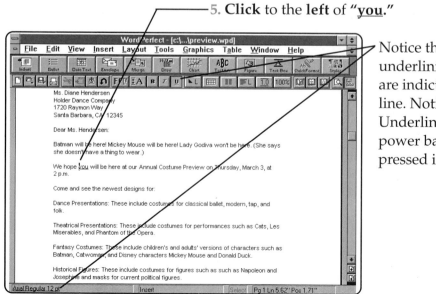

Notice the font, underlining, and point size are indicted in the status line. Notice also that the Underline button in the power bar appears pressed in.

CENTERING TEXT USING THE POWER BAR

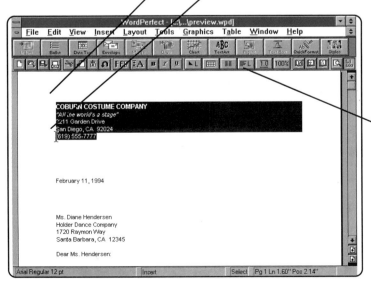

In this section you will center two sections of text. In both cases you will first highlight the lines you want to center.

1. Click on the **Page Up button**. This will take you to the top of the page on which your cursor is located. Your cursor, however, is still located further down the page where you last placed it.

2. Click in the **left margin** next to **"COBURN."** The line will be highlighted.

3. Press and hold the **Shift key** on your keyboard. *With the cursor in the shape of an I-beam*, click to the left of "(619) 555-7777." All the lines between clicks will be highlighted.

4. Place the mouse pointer over the **Justification button**. Notice that it has an L and the lines on the button are aligned on the left to reflect the fact that the highlighted text is left-aligned.

5. Press and hold the mouse button and **drag** the highlight bar down to **Center**.

6. Release the mouse button.

You will now center the second portion of text.

7. Click on the **Page Down button**. This will take you to the top of page two.

8. Click to the **left** of **"Annual Costume Preview."**

9. Press and hold the mouse button and **drag** the highlight bar to the **end of "March 3."**

10. Release the mouse button.

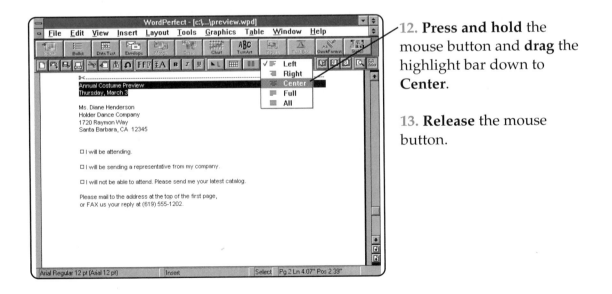

11. Place the mouse pointer over the **Justification button**. Notice there is an L on the button and the lines on the button are aligned on the left.

12. Press and hold the mouse button and **drag** the highlight bar down to **Center**.

13. Release the mouse button.

CENTERING TEXT USING THE LAYOUT MENU

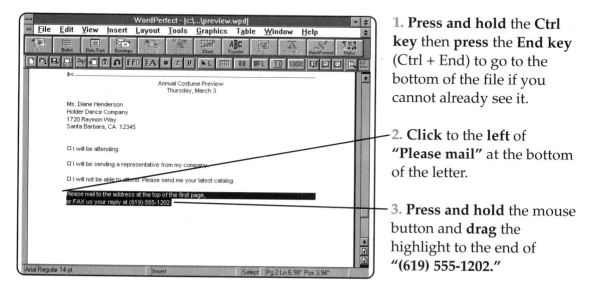

1. **Press and hold** the **Ctrl key** then **press** the **End key** (Ctrl + End) to go to the bottom of the file if you cannot already see it.

2. **Click** to the **left** of **"Please mail"** at the bottom of the letter.

3. **Press and hold** the mouse button and **drag** the highlight to the end of **"(619) 555-1202."**

4. **Click** on **Layout** in the menu bar. A pull-down menu will appear.

5. **Click** on **Justification**. A second menu will appear.

6. **Click** on **Center**. The menus will disappear and your document screen will appear with the highlighted text centered.

UNDOING TEXT ALIGNMENT

In this example you will change text that is center aligned to make it left aligned. Then you will undo the change.

1. Repeat steps 1 and 2 of the **previous section** if the last two lines of the letter are not already highlighted.

2. Place your cursor on the **Layout Justification button**. Notice there is a C on the button and the lines on the button are centered.

3. Press and hold the mouse button and **drag** the highlight up to **Left**.

4. Release the mouse button. The two lines of text will be left aligned.

Since you want the text centered instead of left aligned, you need to undo your last move.

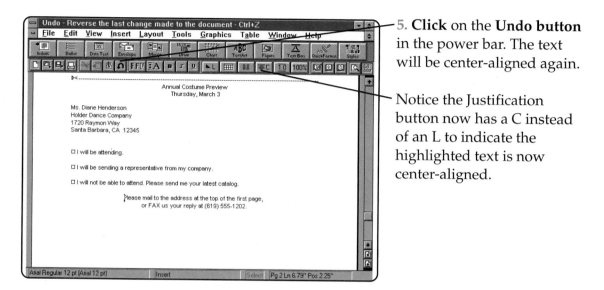

5. Click on the **Undo button** in the power bar. The text will be center-aligned again.

Notice the Justification button now has a C instead of an L to indicate the highlighted text is now center-aligned.

Now would be a good time to save your changes. You should get into the habit of saving while you work.

6. Click on **File** in the menu bar. A pull-down menu will appear.

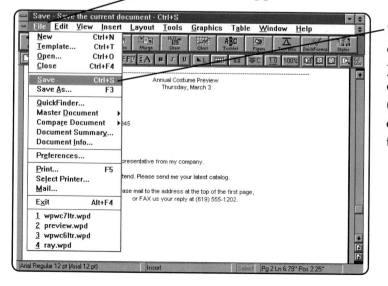

7. Click on **Save**. The changes will be saved and you will be returned to the document screen. (Remember you can also click on the Save button in the power bar.)

ADDING A BORDER
AND SHADING

1. Press and hold the **Ctrl key** and then **press** the **Home key** (Ctrl + Home) to go to the top of the file.

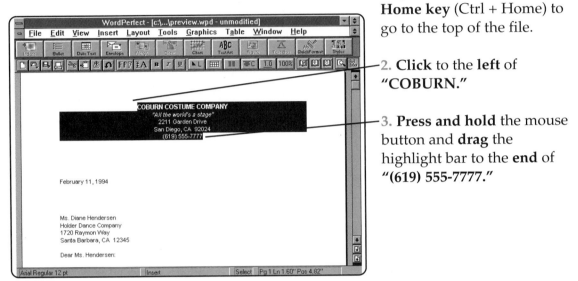

2. Click to the **left** of **"COBURN."**

3. Press and hold the mouse button and **drag** the highlight bar to the **end** of **"(619) 555-7777."**

4. Click on **Layout** in the menu bar. A pull-down menu will appear.

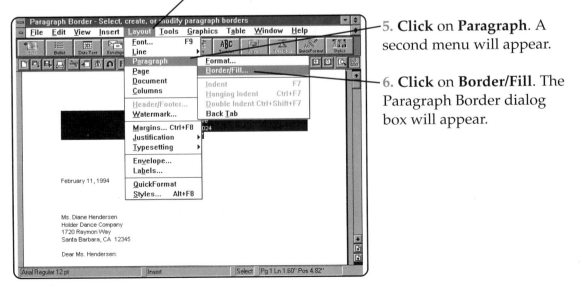

5. Click on **Paragraph**. A second menu will appear.

6. Click on **Border/Fill**. The Paragraph Border dialog box will appear.

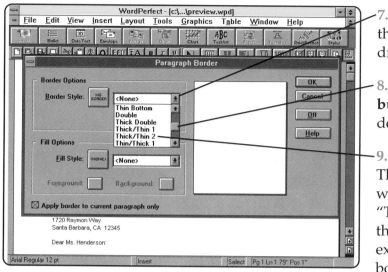

7. Click on the ↓ next to the Border Styles box. A drop down list will appear.

8. Click and drag the **scroll button** in the list **halfway** down the scroll bar.

9. Click on **Thick/Thin2**. The drop down list will disappear and "Thick/Thin2" will be in the Border Styles box. An example of the double border will be displayed on the example sheet.

10. Click on the ↓ next to the Fill Styles box. Your screen will show <None> in the box. A drop down list will appear.

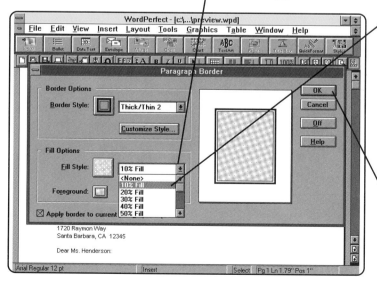

11. Click on **10% Fill**. The drop down list will disappear.

Notice that your selections of a Double border and 10% fill are shown in the Paragraph border dialog box.

12. Click on **OK**. The Paragraph Border dialog box will disappear and your document screen will appear with the border and shading you selected.

13. Click anywhere on the document to get rid of the highlighting.

Your screen will look like this example.

DELETING BORDERS AND SHADING

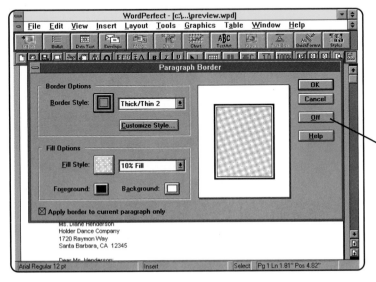

1. Repeat steps 1 through 6 of the previous section to highlight the five lines of type at the top of the page and open the Paragraph Border dialog box.

2. Click on **Off**. You will return to your document screen with the border and fill style removed.

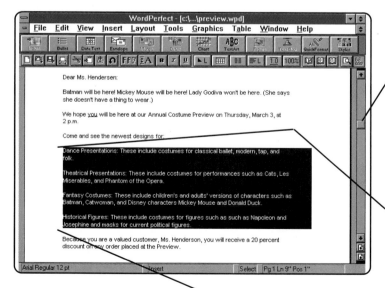

Since you went to the effort to create a shaded border for the company name, you surely don't want to delete it.

3. Click on the **Undo button** on the power bar to undo the removal of the border and shading.

CREATING A BULLETED LIST

In this section, with a few clicks of your mouse, you will create a bulleted list using the four paragraphs describing the costumes carried by the Coburn Costume Company.

1. Drag the **scroll button one quarter** of the way **down** the scroll bar so you can see the paragraphs that describe the newest costume designs.

2. Click in the **left margin** beside **"Dance Presentations."** The paragraph will be highlighted.

3. Press and hold the mouse button and **drag** the cursor **down** to the **"Historical" paragraph**. The four paragraphs will be highlighted.

4. Click on the **Bullet button** in the button bar. The Bullets & Numbers dialog box will appear.

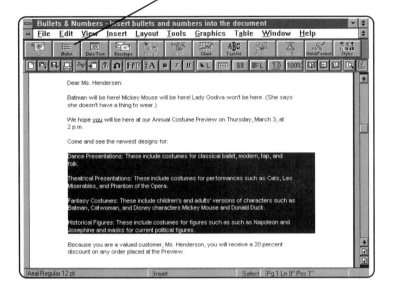

5. Click on **Diamond** to select a diamond-shaped bullet for your bulleted list.

6. Click on **OK**. The Bullets & Numbers dialog box will disappear and the four paragraphs you highlighted will be in the form of a bulleted list. Pretty neat!

7. Click anywhere on the document to remove the highlighting.

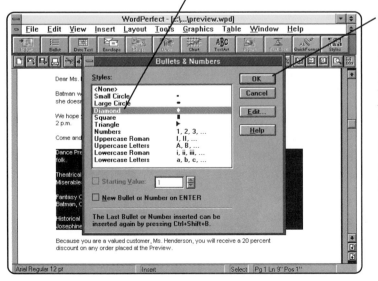

DELETING A BULLET

1. **Click** to the **left** of **"Historical Figures."**

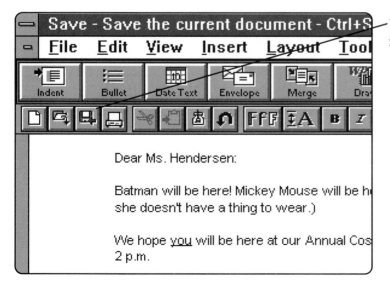

2. **Press** the **Backspace key**. The bullet will be deleted and the paragraph will be aligned at the left margin.

Use the Undo feature to restore the bullet.

3. **Click** on the **Undo button** in the power bar. The bullet will be restored.

SAVING YOUR WORK

You definitely need to save after all this work.

1. **Click** on the **Save button** in the power bar.

Setting Tabs

WordPerfect has tabs preset every half inch. To insert a tab, simply press the Tab key. You can also set your own tabs. When you set a tab, it is set from that point on for the rest of the document until you reset the tabs. You can reset tabs as many times as you like within a document. In this chapter you will change the line spacing to double space and set and apply the following kinds of tabs:

❖ A *left-aligned tab* that aligns words or numbers on the first character: Josh
                                                          Jessica

❖ A *leader* (line) that ends at a right-aligned tab: Josh _____
                                              Jessica ____

❖ A *right-aligned tab* that aligns words or numbers on the last character: Josh
                                                     Jessica

❖ A *center-aligned tab* that centers words or numbers: Josh
                                             Jessica

❖ A *decimal tab* that aligns numbers on the decimal point: 13.95
                                               105.00

DISPLAYING THE RULER BAR

In this example you will display the ruler bar, which is a wonderfully helpful feature when you're setting tabs.

1. **Click** on **View** in the menu bar. A pull-down menu will appear.

2. **Click** on **Ruler Bar**. The ruler bar will appear below the power bar.

Notice the left-aligned tab mark every half-inch.

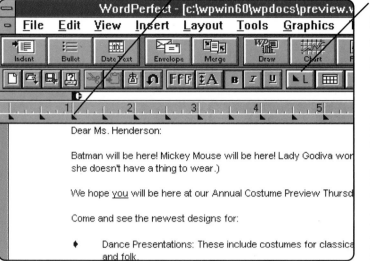

Notice also that the tab button in the power bar shows L, which means it is preset for a left-aligned tab.

RESETTING TABS FOR A BULLETED LIST

In a bulleted list, the paragraph is indented a tab width (the pre-set half inch) to the right of the bullet. You can, however, change the space between the bullet and the paragraph by simply resetting the tab. First, you will clear the existing tabs.

Clearing Existing Tabs

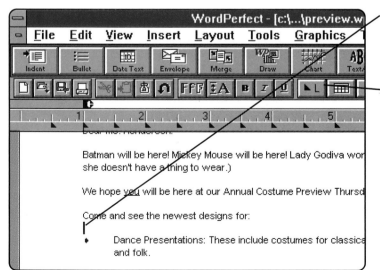

1. Click on the **blank line** above the first bulleted paragraph.

2. Click on the **Tab button** in the power bar. A pull-down menu will appear.

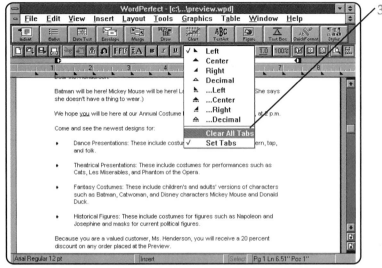

3. **Click** on **Clear All Tabs**.

Notice that the tab marks on the ruler have disappeared.

Notice also that the space between the bullets and the paragraphs has disappeared.

SETTING A LEFT-ALIGNED TAB WITH THE MOUSE

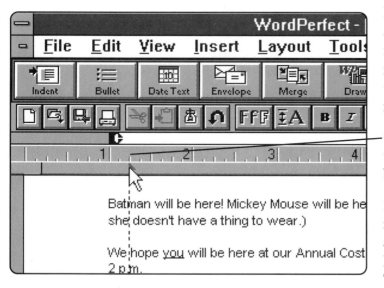

In this example you will set a tab ¼ inch from the left margin. Because the left margin is 1 inch wide, the tab will be set at the 1¼ inch mark on the ruler.

1. **Place** the **mouse arrow** in the lower half of the ruler bar at the 1¼ inch mark.

2. **Press and hold** the **mouse button**. You will see a dotted line appear in your letter at the 1¼ inch mark. The dotted line allows you to check the placement of the tab in relation to the text.

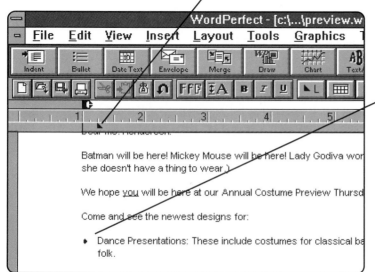

3. **Release** the **mouse button**. A left-aligned tab mark will appear at the 1¼ inch mark. This tab is set for the rest of the document until you change it.

Notice that the bulleted paragraphs are now indented ¼ inch from the left margin.

USING A PRE-SET TAB

In this example you will use the left-aligned tab you set in the last example.

1. Press and hold the **Ctrl key**, then **press** the **End key** (Ctrl + End) to go to the end of the file.

2. Click on the **blank line** above **"I will not be able to attend."** On your screen it will be blank.

3. Press the **Tab key** and **type Name**.

SETTING A RIGHT-ALIGNED TAB

In this section you will use the Tab Set dialog box to insert a solid line (or leader) after "Name." You will use a right-aligned tab to ensure that it ends at a specific spot. This is a three part process.

1. Click on **Layout** in the menu bar. A pull-down menu will appear.

2. Click on **Line**. Another pull-down menu will appear.

3. Click on **Tab Set**. The Tab Set dialog box will appear.

4. Click and hold on **Left** in the Type box. A pull-down menu will appear.

5. Continue to **hold** the mouse button and **drag** the highlight bar down to **Right** then release the mouse button. The pull-down menu will disappear and Right will appear in the type box.

If you wanted a dotted-line leader (like you see in a Table of Contents) you would highlight Dot Right.

6. Place the mouse pointer in the **Position box**. It will be in the shape of an I-beam.

7. Click twice. The 0″ will be highlighted.

8. Type 4. It will replace the highlighted number.

Notice that Left Margin (Relative) is pre-selected (already has a dot in the circle). Relative means the tab is set in relation to the left margin. If you change the left margin, the tab will stay the same distance from the new left margin. An absolute tab, on the other hand, is measured from the edge of the paper. If you change the margin, the distance from the edge of the paper to the tab does not change.

9. Click on **OK**. The dialog box will close.

Now you have a right-aligned tab set at 4 inches. However, you still have to set up the solid line (underline) feature.

10. Click on **Layout** in the menu bar. A pull-down menu will appear.

11. Click on **Font**. The Font dialog box will appear.

Notice the right-aligned tab mark on the ruler at 5 inches. Because the Left Margin (Relative) option was selected when you set the tab, the 4-inch tab is relative to the 1-inch margin and is, therefore, at 5 inches on the ruler. (It seems a little complicated, doesn't it?)

12. Click on **Tabs** to insert a ✕ in the box. This tells WordPerfect to underline tab spaces.

13. Click on **OK**. The dialog box will close.

There's one more step in this process.

The third step in the process is to actually turn on the underline feature.

Combined Position - Display page number, line, position.

File   Edit   View   Insert   Layout   Tools   Graphics

Indent   Bullet   Date Text   Envelope   Merge   Draw   Chart   Text

Annual Costume Preview
Thursday, March 3

Ms. Diane Henderson
Holder Dance Company

14. Click on the **Underline button** in the power bar to turn the underline function on. The button will appear pressed in on your screen. (As long as the Underline button is depressed, tabs will be underlined. You will turn off the underline function in the next section.)

Notice the right-aligned tab mark on the ruler at the 5 inch mark.

Now, you're finally ready to insert the right-aligned leader line.

WordPerfect - [c:\...\preview.wpd]

File   Edit   View   Insert   Layout   Tools   Graphics   Table   Window   Help

Indent   Bullet   Date Text   Envelope   Merge   Draw   Chart   TextArt   Figure   Text Box   QuickFormat   Styles

Annual Costume Preview
Thursday, March 3

Ms. Diane Henderson
Holder Dance Company
1720 Raymon Way
Santa Barbara, CA 12345

☐ I will be attending.

☐ I will be sending a representative from my company.
Name_____

☐ I will not be able to attend. Please send me your latest catalog.

Please mail to the address at the top of the first page,

Arial Regular 12 pt   Insert   Select   Pg 2 Ln 6.39" Pos 1"

15. Press the **Tab key** on your keyboard. The leader will be inserted into the text.

16. Press Enter to move the insertion point to a new line.

SETTING AN EXACT TAB

When you set a tab with the mouse, it may or may not be at an exact position. You may get a tab at .244 inches, for example, rather than .25 inches. In most cases this difference doesn't matter. If you need to set a tab at a precise position, however, use the Tab Set dialog box.

In this example you will set a left-aligned tab at precisely .5 inches.

1. **Click twice** on **any tab mark** in the ruler. This is another way to open the Tab Set dialog box.

2. **Click twice** in the **Position box**. The 0" in the box will be highlighted.

3. **Type .5** to set the tab at exactly ½ inch. It will replace the 0".

4. Confirm that Left is in the Type box.

5. **Click** on **OK**. The dialog box will close.

6. Click on the **Underline button** in the power bar. Because the underline function is turned on when the button is pressed in, clicking on the button again will turn off the underline function.

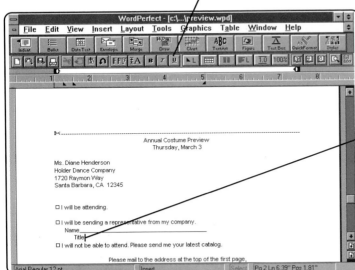

7. Press the **Tab key** on your keyboard twice to tab to the ½ inch mark.

8. Type Title.

Now you have to turn the underline function on once again.

9. Click on the **Underline button** in the power bar to turn it on. The button will appear pressed in on your screen.

10. Press the **Tab key** on your keyboard. You will tab to the next tab position, which is a right-aligned tab at the 5-inch mark.

11. Press Enter to move the insertion point to the next line.

DELETING A TAB

In this example you will delete the tab you set at the .5-inch mark.

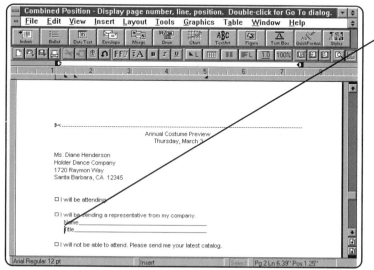

1. Click to the **left** of **Title** to set the cursor. On your screen it will be indented to the ½ inch mark.

2. Press the **Backspace key** on your keyboard. The word "Title" will be backspaced to align under "Name." Notice that the underline automatically extends to the right-aligned tab at 5 inches.

3. Click and hold on the ½ **inch tab mark** in the ruler bar.

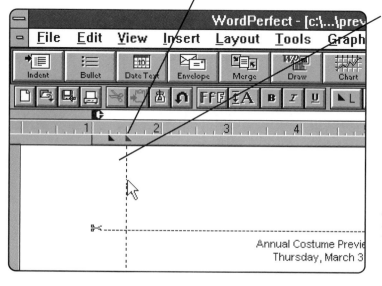

4. Continue to hold the **mouse button** and **drag** the tab marker down into the document page.

5. Release the mouse button. The tab will be removed from the ruler bar. (Isn't this a really cool feature!)

6. Press and hold the **Ctrl key** then **type** the letter **s** (Ctrl + s) to save your work. (This is another way to save.)

OPENING A NEW DOCUMENT

In the remaining sections of this chapter, you'll review setting right-aligned tabs. You will also learn how to set a center-aligned tab and a decimal tab. Since the tabs will not be used in the preview.wpd letter, you will open a new document. You don't need to close preview.wpd in order to open a new document. WordPerfect allows up to nine documents to be open at a time.

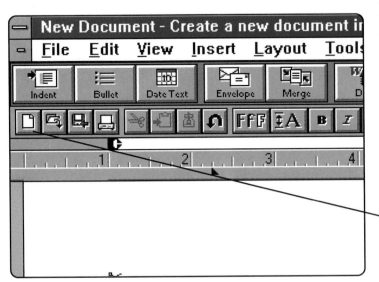

1. **Click** on the **New Document button** in the power bar. A new document screen will appear

SETTING A RIGHT-ALIGNED TAB

Notice that a new document does not have a ruler bar.

1. **Click** on **View** in the menu bar. A pull-down menu will appear.

2. **Click** on **Ruler Bar**. The ruler bar will appear.

3. **Click and hold** the **mouse button** on the Tab button in the power bar. A pull-down list will appear.

4. Continue to **hold** the mouse button and **drag** the highlight bar down to **Clear All Tabs**. Then release the mouse button.

Now that you have all the tabs cleared, you are ready to tell WordPerfect that the next tab should be a right-aligned tab.

5. Click and hold on the **Tab button** in the power bar once again. The pull-down list will appear.

6. Continue to **hold** the mouse button and **drag** the highlight bar down to **Right**. Then release the mouse button. An R will appear on the face of the Tab button.

7. **Place** the mouse arrow at the **1¹/₂ inch mark** on the ruler bar and **click** to set the tab. You will see a dotted line appear as you hold down the mouse button. A right-aligned tab mark will appear at the 1½ inch mark.

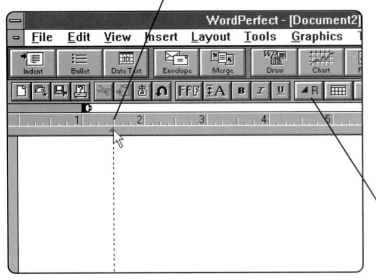

SETTING A CENTER-ALIGNED TAB

First, you must set the Tab button in the power bar for a center-aligned tab.

1. **Click and hold** on the **Tab button** in the power bar. A pull-down list will appear.

2. **Continue** to **hold** the mouse button and **drag** the highlight bar to **Center** then release the mouse button. A C will appear on the button face and the next tab you set will be a center-aligned tab.

3. **Place** the mouse pointer at the **3-inch mark** on the ruler and **click** to set the tab. A center-aligned tab mark will appear in the ruler bar.

SETTING DECIMAL TABS

In this section you will set two decimal tabs. First, you will set the Tab button in the power bar for decimal tabs.

1. **Click and hold** on the **Tab button** in the power bar. A pull-down list will appear.

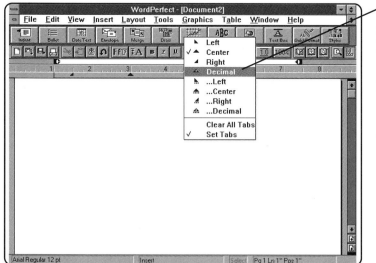

2. **Continue** to **hold** the mouse button and **drag** the highlight bar down to **Decimal**. Then **release** the mouse button. The pull-down menu will disappear and a D will appear on the button face.

3. Place the mouse pointer at the **4½ inch mark** on the ruler bar and click to set the tab. The letter D will appear on the button face.

4. Place the mouse arrow at the **6-inch mark** on the ruler bar and **click** to set a second decimal tab.

CHANGING LINE SPACING

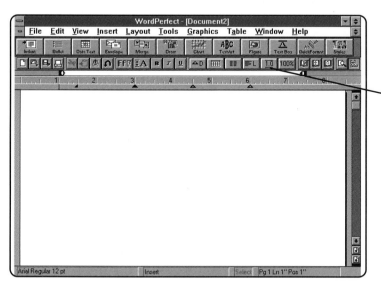

In this section you will change the line spacing from single to double.

1. Click and hold on the **Line Spacing button** on the power bar. A pull-down list will appear.

2. Continue to hold the mouse button and **drag** the highlight bar down to **2.0** and release the mouse button. The line spacing of this new document will change to double spacing.

APPLYING TABS

In this section you will apply the tabs you set in the previous sections. Notice how each text entry aligns on the tabs you set.

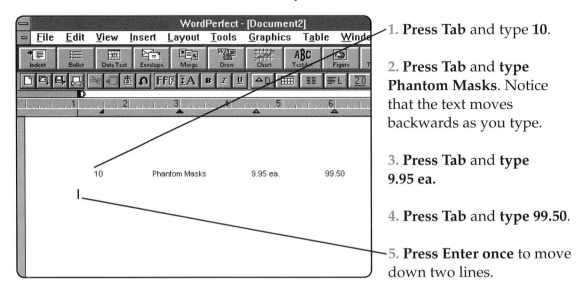

1. **Press Tab** and type **10**.

2. **Press Tab** and **type Phantom Masks**. Notice that the text moves backwards as you type.

3. **Press Tab** and **type 9.95 ea.**

4. **Press Tab** and **type 99.50**.

5. **Press Enter once** to move down two lines.

6. **Press Tab** and **type 5**. Notice the "5" is right-aligned under "10."

7. **Press Tab** and **type Catwoman Costumes**. Notice that it is centered under the entry above it.

8. **Press Tab** and **type 95.00 ea.** Notice that the decimal points are lined up.

9. **Press Tab** and **type 475.00**. Again, notice the decimal points are aligned.

SWITCHING BETWEEN OPEN DOCUMENTS

In this section you will switch back and forth between the unnamed file on your screen and preview.wpd.

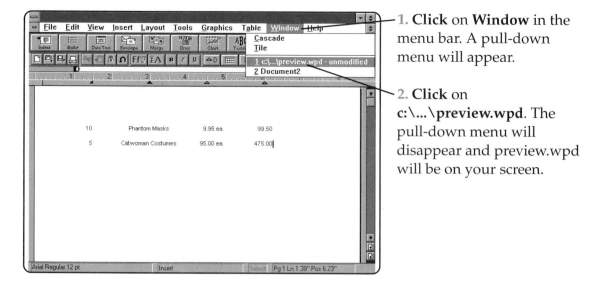

1. **Click** on **Window** in the menu bar. A pull-down menu will appear.

2. **Click** on **c:\...\preview.wpd**. The pull-down menu will disappear and preview.wpd will be on your screen.

3. **Click** on **Window** in the menu bar. A pull-down menu will appear.

4. **Click** on **Document2**. The pull-down menu will disappear and the document with the tabs will be on your screen.

CLOSING WITHOUT SAVING

Since the previous tab examples were meant only as practice in setting different types of tabs and will not be used later in the book, you don't need to save the document.

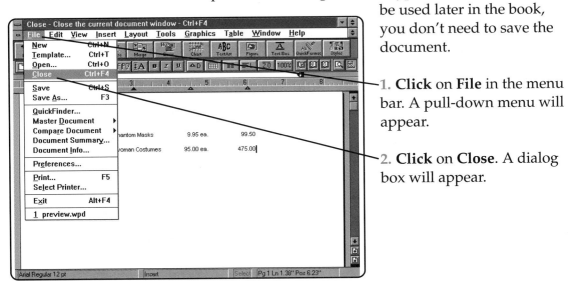

1. **Click** on **File** in the menu bar. A pull-down menu will appear.

2. **Click** on **Close**. A dialog box will appear.

3. **Click** on **No**. The file will close without being saved. Since you never saved this document to begin with, it will simply disappear.

Closing without saving is a handy trick to remember if you have made changes to your document that you don't like. Closing without saving will cause a previously saved document to revert to what it was the last time you saved it.

REMOVING THE RULER BAR

The ruler is useful for doing tasks such as tabs. However, it takes up quite a bit of your screen space. For this reason we recommend you remove it when you're not using it.

1. **Click** on **View** in the menu bar. A pull-down menu will appear.

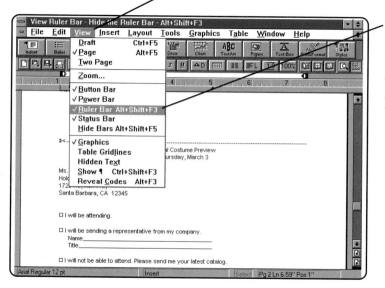

2. **Click** on **Ruler Bar**. The pull-down menu will disappear and the ruler bar will no longer be visible on your screen.

Adding a Header and a Page Number

A header or footer is information that is printed at the top or bottom of a page, respectively. For example, in this book the page number and book title is a header on every left page and the chapter number and title and page number is a header on every right page. In this chapter you will do the following:

❖ Change the margin on page 2 of the preview.wpd sample document

❖ Insert a header on page 2

❖ Insert a page number on page 2

CHANGING THE MARGIN

In WordPerfect you can change margins as many times as you want within a document. Each time you make a change, the new margin applies in the document until you change it again. In this example you will change the top margin on the second page to make space for a header. First, you must go to the spot where you want the change to begin.

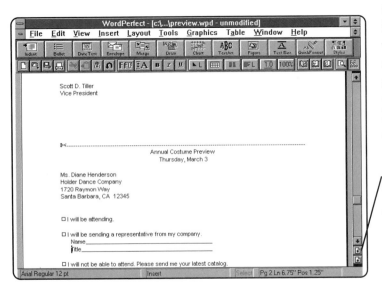

1. Click on the **Page Up button**. This will bring you to the top of page two.

Notice that your screen shows the top of page 2. The screen does not show the cursor at the top of page 2 because the Page Up button does not move the cursor.

2. **Click** on the **Page Up button** again. This will move the screen to the top of page 1.

3. **Click** on the **Page Down button** to show the top of page 2.

4. **Click** to the **left** of **"Please return..."** to set the cursor because the margin reset command works from wherever the cursor is.

5. **Click** on **Layout** in the menu bar. A pull-down menu will appear.

6. **Click** on **Margins**. the Margins dialog box will appear.

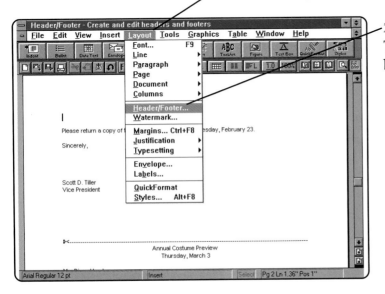

7. Click twice in the **Top box**. The **".800"** will be highlighted.

8. Type 1.

9. Click on **OK**. The document screen will appear with the second page now having a 1-inch top margin.

ADDING A HEADER

In this section you will create a header for page 2 using the words "Ms. Diane Henderson" and the date. Your cursor should be at the top of page 2.

1. Click on **Layout**. A pull-down menu will appear.

2. Click on **Header/Footer**. The Header/Footer dialog box will appear.

Notice that Header A is already selected.

3. Click on **Create**. You will be returned to your document screen and the header bar will appear on your screen below the power bar.

—4. **Type Ms. Diane Henderson** and **press** the **Enter key.**

5. **Click** on the **Date Text button**. Today's date will be inserted at the cursor.

6. **Click** on the **Distance button**. The Distance dialog box will appear.

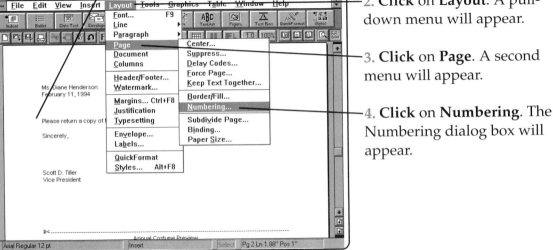

7. **Type .5**. It will replace the highlighted number.

8. **Click** on **OK**. The distance between your header and the first line of text on page 2 will increase to .5.

9. **Click** on **Close** to exit the header.

INSERTING A PAGE NUMBER

To insert a page number, the cursor must be on the page where you want the page numbering to begin.

1. **Click** next to **"Please"** to make sure you are not in the header.

2. **Click** on **Layout**. A pull-down menu will appear.

3. **Click** on **Page**. A second menu will appear.

4. **Click** on **Numbering**. The Numbering dialog box will appear.

5. **Click and hold** on the button labeled **No Page Numbering**.

6. **Drag** the highlight down to **Bottom Center**.

7. **Release** the mouse button.

8. **Click** on **OK**.

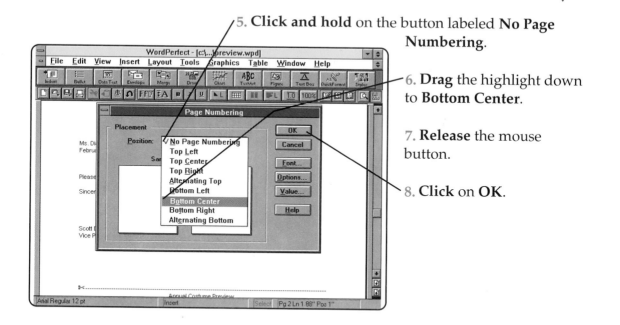

To see the page number you will have to go to the bottom of your page.

9. **Click and hold** on the **scroll button** and **drag** the scroll button to the **bottom** of the **scroll bar**. The page number will be visible.

10. **Press and hold** the **Ctrl key** then **press** the letter **s** (Ctrl + s) to save the changes.

Changing the View

In Chapters 1 through 9 you've been working in the Page view which is the standard, or default, view in WordPerfect 6. This is one of the best views for everyday work. You can, however, change the view of your document so you can see two pages on your screen at the same time or zoom in to show a wide variety of other views. In this chapter you will learn how to show the following views:

❖ Two Page view

❖ Draft view

❖ Full Page view

❖ Page Width view

SHOWING TWO PAGES ON THE SCREEN AT THE SAME TIME

You can see a bird's-eye view of both pages at the same time in the Two Page view.

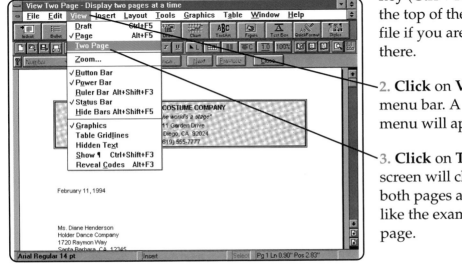

1. **Press and hold** the **Ctrl key** then **press** the **Home key** (Ctrl + Home) to go to the top of the preview.wpd file if you are not already there.

2. **Click** on **View** in the menu bar. A pull-down menu will appear.

3. **Click** on **Two Page**. Your screen will change to show both pages at the same time, like the example on the next page.

This is the Two Page view of your document. You can edit in this view if you can see well enough. Realistically, however, you are pretty much limited to changing page breaks, margins, and paragraphs.

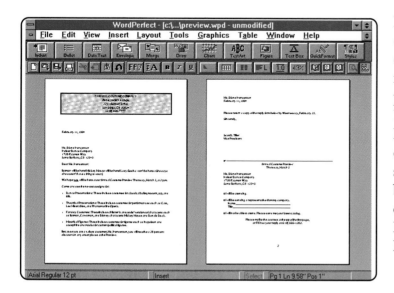

If you had a three-page document, you would see only two pages at a time. To move to page 3, click on page 2, then press the **Page Down key** on your keyboard. Page 2 will show on the left and page 3 will show on the right. To go back to pages 1 and 2, click on page 2, then press the **Page Up key** on your keyboard.

DRAFT VIEW

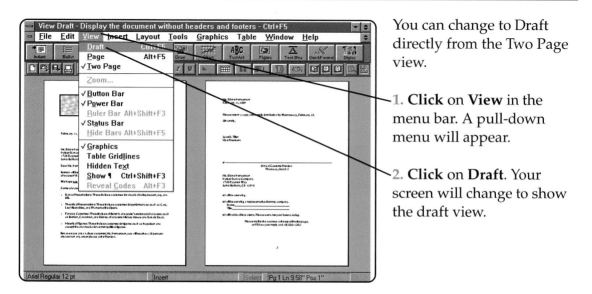

You can change to Draft directly from the Two Page view.

1. **Click** on **View** in the menu bar. A pull-down menu will appear.

2. **Click** on **Draft**. Your screen will change to show the draft view.

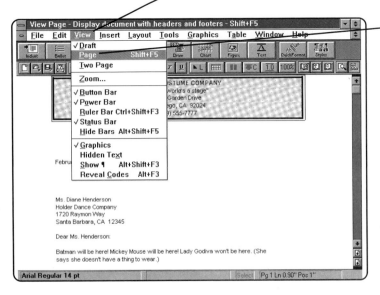

The Draft view is faster to work in because the display is not as good as Page view. Also, you do not see headers, footers, or page numbers in Draft view.

In the next section you will switch back to the Page view before switching to Zoom.

ZOOM VIEW

First you will switch back to Page view.

1. Click on **View** in the menu bar. A pull-down menu will appear.

2. Click on **Page**. You will be returned to the Page view.

3. **Click** on **View** in the menu bar. A pull-down menu will appear.

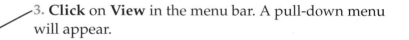

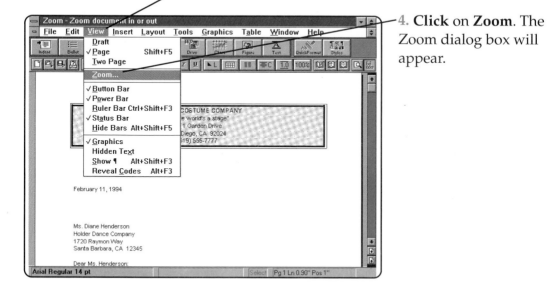

4. **Click** on **Zoom**. The Zoom dialog box will appear.

FULL PAGE VIEW

1. **Click** on **Full Page** to insert a dot in the circle.

2. **Click** on **OK**. The screen will change to show the Full Page view.

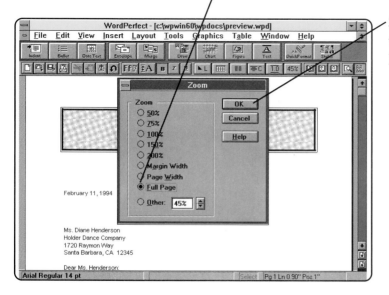

The full page view is another bird's-eye view of the document.

3. **Click** on the **Page Down button** on the scroll bar to see page 2.

This is page 2 of the document.

You can access the options in the Zoom dialog box by using a button on the power bar.

4. **Place** the mouse arrow on the **Zoom button**. Notice that the button shows what percentage this page is of the Full Page view. In this example, it is 45%, but yours may be different.

PAGE WIDTH VIEW

1. **Click and hold** the mouse button on the **Zoom button**. A pull-down menu will appear.

2. **Continue** to **hold** the mouse button and **drag** the highlight bar down to Page Width.

3. **Release** the mouse button. The screen will change to show the Page Width view.

This is the Page Width view. It shows a slightly larger view of the document than the Page view.

SWITCHING BACK TO PAGE VIEW

You can switch back to the standard view by using the Zoom button on the power bar again.

1. **Place** the **mouse arrow** on the **Zoom button** on the power bar.

2. **Click and hold** the mouse arrow on the Zoom button. A pull-down menu will appear.

3. **Continue** to **hold** the mouse button and **drag** the highlight bar to 100%.

4. **Release** the mouse button. The screen will change to show the standard 100% view.

Try experimenting with different views.

Program Manager

Part III Printing an Envelope

Printing an Envelope

WordPerfect 6 has an Envelope button to make it easy to set up and print an envelope. In this chapter you will do the following:

❖ Use the Envelope button to print a standard business envelope with a preprinted return address on an HP LaserJet Series II or III printer and on a dot-matrix printer

❖ Customize the envelope text

❖ Print a letter with an attached envelope

USING THE ENVELOPE BUTTON TO PRINT

In this section you will print a standard business envelope with a preprinted return address using the manual feed feature of your printer.

(**Note:** You will learn how to print multiple envelopes using an envelope tray in Chapter 16 in the section entitled, "Setting Up WordPerfect to Use an Envelope Tray.") After you complete the steps below, refer to the directions for either HP Laser-Jet Series II or III printers (and printers that emulate them) or dot-matrix printers.

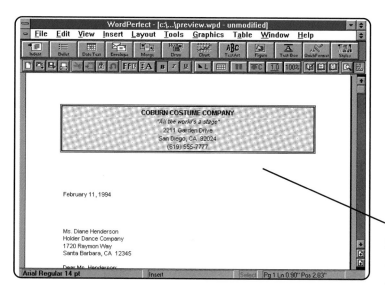

1. **Open** the **PREVIEW** file if it is not already on your screen. Your cursor can be anywhere in the letter.

2. **Click** on the **Envelope button** in the Button Bar. The Envelope dialog box will appear with Ms. Diane Henderson's name and address on the sample envelope.

(If you did not install a WordPerfect driver, you will see a Create Envelope Definitions dialog box. Make whatever changes are necessary, then click on OK.)

Printing with an HP Laserjet II or III Series Printer

Notice that Diane Henderson's name and mailing address now appears in the Mailing Addresses text box and on the sample envelope. (Pretty clever of the WordPerfect programmers, don't you think!)

1. **Place a single envelope in the manual feed slot** on your printer's paper tray. Since each brand of printer operates slightly differently, see your printer's manual for the exact placement of the envelope as you feed it into the printer.

2. **Click** on **Print Envelope**.

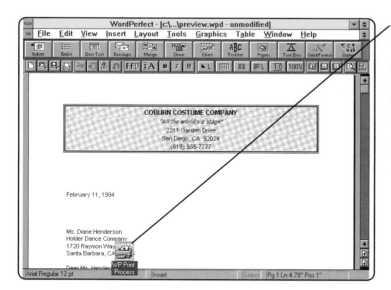

A print message box will briefly appear on your screen and the WordPerfect Printer icon will appear. Check your printer's manual to see if you have to press a Form Feed or similar button. Then your envelope will begin to print.

Printing with a Dot-Matrix Printer

1. Remove the **tractor feed paper** from your printer and **insert** an **envelope**. If you want the return address to be printed farther down on the envelope, position it manually before printing. Your printer may allow you to feed an envelope without removing the tractor feed paper. Check your printer's manual for help.

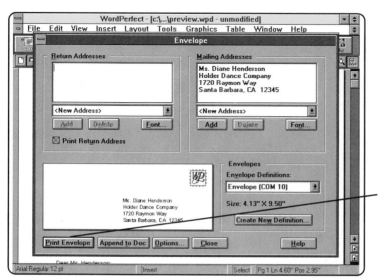

2. Click on **Print Envelope**.

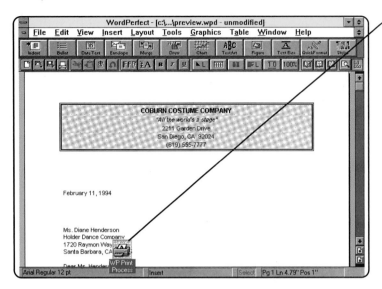

A print message box will briefly appear on your screen and you will see the WordPerfect printer icon. Then your envelope will begin to print.

ADDING THE RETURN ADDRESS TO THE ENVELOPE

Although WordPerfect automatically shows the mailing address of the letter in the Envelope dialog box, you have to type in the return address.

1. **Click** on the **Envelope button** in the button bar. The Envelope dialog box will appear.

2. Click in the **left corner** of the **Return Address box** to set the insertion point.

3. Type the return address (**press Enter** after each line):

COBURN COSTUME COMPANY
"All the world's a stage"
2211 Garden drive
San Diego, CA 92024

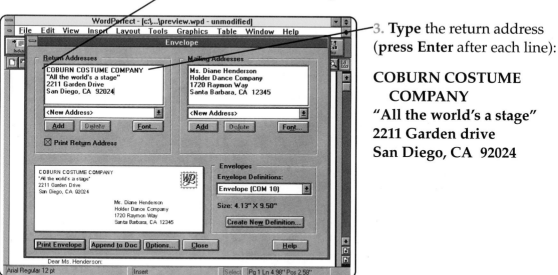

4. Click on the **Add button** to save this address.

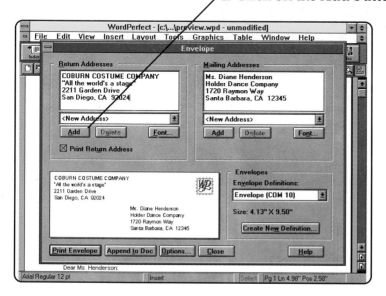

PRINTING THE RETURN ADDRESS

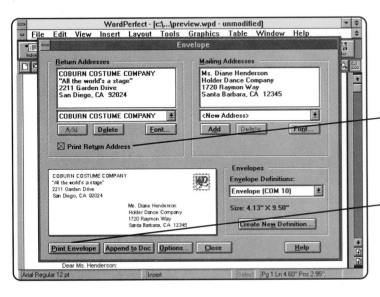

Place a single envelope in your printer's paper tray or tractor feed. See the previous sections if you need help.

1. Click on **Print Return Address** to insert an X in the box if one is not already there.

2. Click on the **Print Envelope button**. The envelope will begin printing after a printing message box appears briefly.

ADDING A NEW RETURN ADDRESS

When you click on the Envelope button, WordPerfect will display the last return address you used. In this example you will add a new return address.

1. Click on the **Envelope button** in the button bar. The Envelope dialog box will appear.

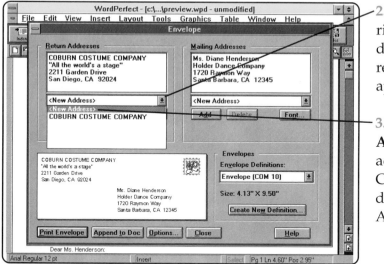

2. Click on the ⬇ to the right of <New Address>. A drop-down list of saved return addresses will appear.

3. Click on <**New Address**>. The return address for COBURN COSTUME COMPANY will disappear from the Return Addresses text box above.

4. Click in the **Return Addresses text box** to set the cursor.

5. Type the following return address:

**Mr. David A. Coburn
1 Daggett Road
La Jolla, CA 54321**

6. Click on **Add**.

7. Click on **Print Envelope**. Because WordPerfect remembers the last return address you printed, the David Coburn address will be shown as the return address in the Envelope dialog box the next time you click on the Envelope button.

CHANGING TO A
DIFFERENT RETURN ADDRESS

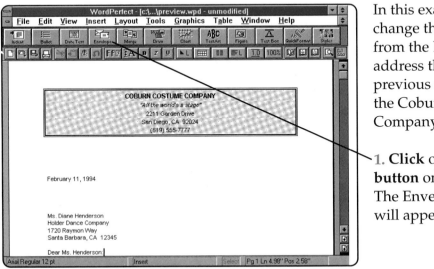

In this example you will change the return address from the David Coburn address that printed on the previous envelope back to the Coburn Costume Company address.

1. Click on the **Envelope button** on the button bar. The Envelope dialog box will appear.

2. Click on the ⬇ to the right of the New Address text box.

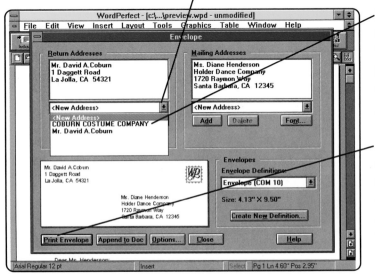

3. Click on **COBURN COSTUME COMPANY**. The COBURN COSTUME COMPANY return address will appear in the Return Addresses text box.

4. Click on **Print Envelope**. COBURN COSTUME COMPANY will show as the return address the next time you open this dialog box.

CUSTOMIZING THE ENVELOPE TEXT

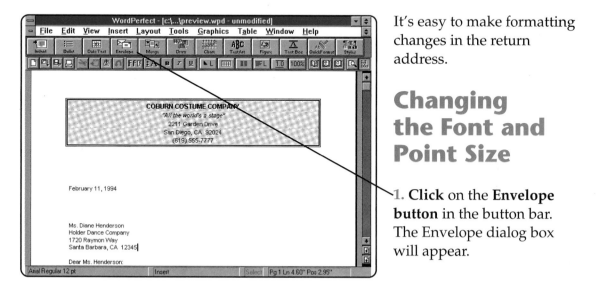

It's easy to make formatting changes in the return address.

Changing the Font and Point Size

1. Click on the **Envelope button** in the button bar. The Envelope dialog box will appear.

2. Click to the **left** of **"COBURN"** in the Return Addresses box to set the cursor.

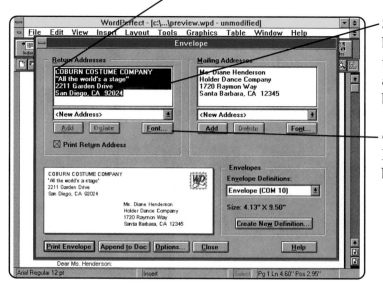

3. Press and hold the mouse button and **drag** the cursor to **highlight** the return address. **Release** the mouse button.

4. Click on **Font**. The Return Address Font dialog box will appear.

Arial will be highlighted in the Font Faces list because it is the font for the current document.

5. Click on the ⬇ on the scroll bar to scroll down the list of available fonts to CG Times. Choose another font if you do have this one.

6. Click on **CG Times**.

7. Click on **10** in the Font Size box.

8. Click on **OK**. The Envelope Dialog box will reappear.

Don't panic! You won't see the changes made to the envelope until it is printed.

Making the First Line of the Address Bold

1. Click to the **left** of **"COBURN"** to set the cursor.

2. Press and hold the mouse button as you **drag** the cursor to highlight the company name. **Release** the mouse button.

3. Click on **Font**. The Return Address Font dialog box will appear.

4. Click on **Bold** to insert an X in the box.

5. Click on **OK**. The Envelope dialog box will reappear.

6. Click on **Print Envelope**.

PRINTING A LETTER WITH AN ATTACHED ENVELOPE

Attaching an Envelope to a Letter

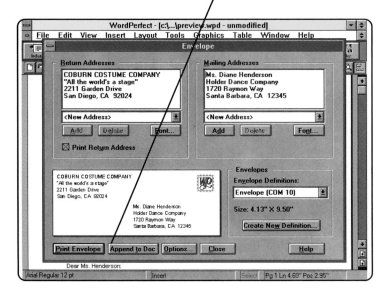

1. Click on the **Envelope button**. The Envelope dialog box will appear.

2. Click on **Append to Doc**.

Notice that the newly attached envelope will appear as page 3 of the letter.

3. Click on the **Print button** in the button bar. The Print dialog box will appear.

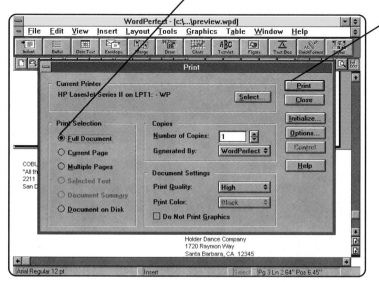

4. Click on **Full Document** to insert a dot in the circle if it does not already have one.

5. Click on **Print**. The WordPerfect message box will appear briefly. WordPerfect will print both the envelope and the letter. (Check your printer's manual to see if you need to press Form Feed or any other special button.)

PRINTING AN ATTACHED ENVELOPE WITHOUT A LETTER

1. Click on the **Envelope document** to set the cursor.

2. Click on the **Print button** in the power bar. The Print dialog box will appear.

3. Click on **Current Page** to insert a dot in the circle.

4. Click on **Print**.

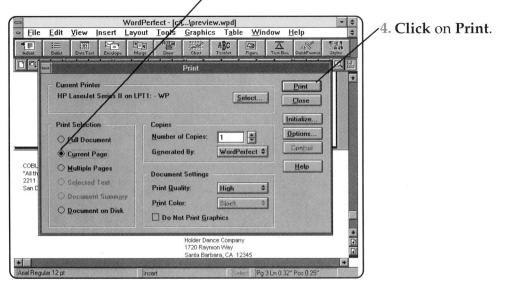

PRINTING A LETTER WITHOUT AN ATTACHED ENVELOPE

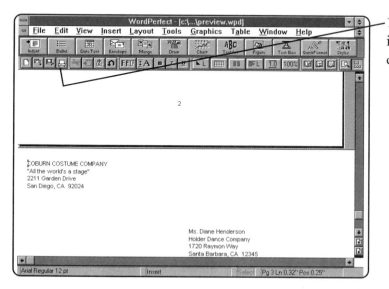

1. Click on the **Print button** in the power bar. The Print dialog box will appear.

2. Click on **Multiple Pages** to insert a dot in the circle.

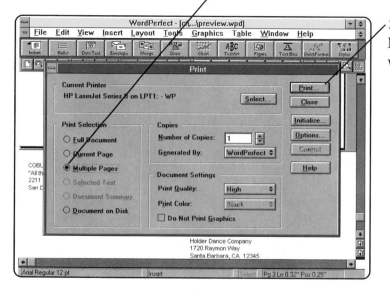

3. Click on **Print**. The Multiple Pages dialog box will appear.

4. Type 1-2 in the page(s) text box. It will replace the highlighted "all" that was there when you opened the dialog box.

5. Click on **Print**. The two page letter will print. The envelope will not print.

CLOSING A LETTER WITHOUT SAVING AN ATTACHED ENVELOPE

1. Click on **File** in the menu bar. A pull-down menu will appear.

2. Click on **Close**. The Save message box will appear and ask if you want to save the changes to your document.

3. Click on **No**.

The letter will close and the envelope will not be attached when you reopen the letter in later chapters.

Creating a Mailing List

With the WordPerfect 6 Merge feature, you can send the same letter to different people and have the individual's name, address, salutation, and other information personalized on each letter without having to retype each letter. After you've written the letter, you begin the merge process by creating a mailing list, as shown in this chapter. Then you edit the mailing list (Chapter 13), attach, code, and print the letters (Chapter 14 and 15). Finally you print personalized envelopes (Chapter 16).

If you have a mailing list already created in another word-processing program, such as WordStar, go to Chapter 17, "Converting a Mailing List," to convert your mailing list to WordPerfect. In this chapter you will do the following:

❖ Create a data entry table

❖ Create a mailing list

SETTING UP A MAILING LIST

To create a mailing list, you must first enter the information for your mailing list into a *data entry table*. Since address information varies in length, reducing the point size of the text used to type the list allows you to see even fairly long entries on your screen.

Changing Font Size

1. **Click** on **Layout** in the menu bar. A pull-down menu will appear.

2. **Click** on **Font**. The Font dialog box will appear.

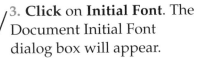

3. Click on **Initial Font**. The Document Initial Font dialog box will appear.

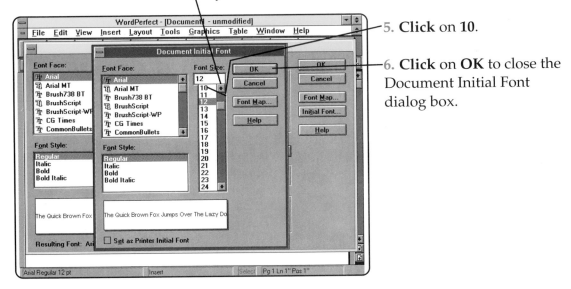

4. Click twice on the ⬆ on the Font Size scroll bar so you can see 10.

5. Click on **10**.

6. Click on **OK** to close the Document Initial Font dialog box.

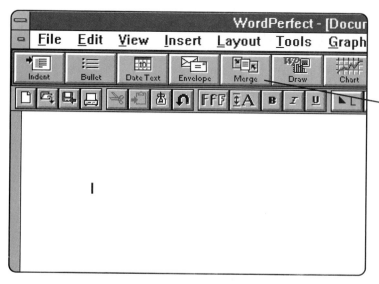

7. Click on **OK** to close the Font dialog box. Your font for the text and the table you will insert in this document are now set at 10 point Arial.

Opening a Data Table

When you create a mailing list, you can tell WordPerfect to show the data in a list format or in a table format. In our experience, mailing lists are much easier to read and edit if they are in a table format. Therefore, in this example, you will tell WordPerfect to create a table to hold your mailing list information.

1. Click on the **Merge button** in the button bar. The Merge dialog box will appear.

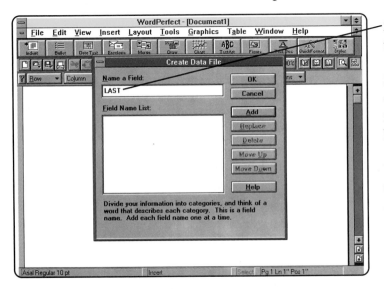

2. Click on **Place Records in a Table** to place an ✕ in the box.

3. Click on **Data**. The Create Data File dialog box will appear.

ENTERING FIELD NAMES

Field names identify specific kinds of data, such as last names, first names, etc. You don't have to type the field names in upper-case letters as shown in the examples in this section. However, the field names will become headings in the table and will stand out better if they are in upper-case letters.

1. Press the **Caps Lock key** on your keyboard to turn on the capital letter function.

2. Type the word **LAST** in the Field Name text box.

3. Press the **Enter key** (or click on Add). "LAST" will move to the Field Name List box below.

Warning: Do not click on OK, or you will end up creating a one-column mailing list of last names only! If this happens, start over again.

4. Type the word **FIRST** in the Field Name List.

5. Press the **Enter key.** "FIRST" will move down to the Field Name List box.

6. Repeat steps 4 and 5 to enter the following words (field names) in the Field Name List box:

STREET
CITY
STATE
ZIP

7. Click on **OK**. The Quick Data Entry dialog box will appear.

ENTERING DATA IN A MAILING LIST WITH QUICK DATA ENTRY

There are two ways to enter data in a list. In this example you will use a dialog box.

Notice that the cursor is flashing in the LAST field box.

1. Type Chambers. (Make sure you have pressed the Caps Lock key to turn the capital letters function off. If you forgot, simply press the Backspace key to erase CHAMBERS and type the word again.)

2. Press the **Enter key** to move to the next box.

3. Type the following words in the FIRST, STREET, CITY, STATE, AND ZIP boxes respectively: (Remember to press Enter after each entry.)

Jane
2211 River St.
Greatplace
VA
02211

If you were going to enter another name, or record, you would click on New Record. In this example you will enter just this one record for Jane Chambers.

4. Click on **Close**. The Quick Data Entry dialog box will close and WordPerfect will ask if you want to save the changes you have made.

WordPerfect - [Document1 - unmodified]

Quick Data Entry

Record

LAST   Chambers
FIRST   Jane
STREET   2211 River St.
CITY   Greatplace
STATE   VA
ZIP   02211

Next Field
Previous Field
New Record
Close
Delete Record
Find...
Field Names...
Help

First Previous Next Last

Press Ctrl+Enter to add a new line at the insertion point.
Edit Fields with Functions

Arial Regular 10 pt   Insert   Select Pg 1 Ln 1" Pos 1"

5. **Click** on **Yes**. The Save Data File As dialog box will appear.

6. **Type mylist** in the Filename box.

7. **Click** on **OK**. The mailing list table will appear on your screen.

ENTERING DATA DIRECTLY INTO A MAILING LIST TABLE

In the previous section you used the Quick Data Entry dialog box to enter data into the mailing list table. In this section you will enter data directly into the table.

Notice that the first row of the table contains the field names. This row is called the *header row*.

Adding a Blank Row to the Table

1. While the cursor is in the last cell of the table, **press the Tab key**. This will add a blank row to the table.

2. **Click** in the first cell of the last line to place the cursor.

3. **Type** the following five fields in the table. Press the Tab key to move to each new cell:

Avery
James
3 Tar Hill Drive
Gardenia
NC
01934

SAVING CHANGES TO A MAILING LIST

Now that you have added a record to the data list, you'll want to save the list again.

1. Click on the **Save button** on the power bar.

LAST	FIRST	STREET
Chambers	Jane	2211 River St.

If you plan to follow along with the next chapter, do not exit the file.

WordPerfect - [c:\wpwin60\wpdocs\mylist - unmodified]

File Edit View Insert Layout Tools Graphics Table Window Help

LAST	FIRST	STREET	CITY	STATE	ZIP
Chambers	Jane	2211 River St.	Greatplace	VA	02211
Avery	James	3 Tar Hill Drive	Gardenia	NC	01934

Arial Regular 10 pt   Insert   Select   Pg 1 Ln 1.85" Pos 1"

Editing a Mailing List

Suppose you created and saved a mailing list, as you did in Chapter 12, and then discover that you didn't include fields for a company name and a person's title, for example. In WordPerfect 6 it is easy to make additions to your mailing list. First you will add the new fields to the list and then add data into the new fields. After that, it is a simple task to resize the cells to make the list more readable. In this chapter you will do the following:

❖ Add fields to the mailing list

❖ Add data into the new fields

❖ Add a new record to the mailing list

❖ Resize the mailing list columns

❖ Save the mailing list

ADDING FIELDS TO THE MAILING LIST

In this section you will add two field headings to the data entry table.

1. Open the **MYLIST** file that you created in Chapter 12 if it is not already open.

2. Click on the **first cell** in the table (LAST) to place the cursor.

3. Click on **Quick Entry** in the Mail Merge toolbar. The Quick Data Entry dialog box will appear.

General Status - Display info for columns, tables, macros, merge, paragraph styles, etc.

File   Edit   View   Insert   Layout   Tools   Graphics   Table   Window   Help

LAST	FIRST	STREET	CITY	STATE	ZIP
Chambers	Jane	2211 River St.	Greatplace	VA	02411
Avery	James	3 Tar Hill Drive	Gardenia	NC	01934

Arial Regular 10 pt   TABLE A Cell A1"   Select   Pg 1 Ln 1.08" Pos 1.08"

Notice that the fields and first record of the mylist table appears in the dialog box. If you had clicked on another row, a different record would show.

4. Click on **Field Names**. The Edit Field Names dialog box will appear.

Notice that the cursor is flashing in the field Name text box.

5. Type PREFIX (in capital letters) in the Field Name text box.

6. Click on **Add Before**. PREFIX will be added to the top of the list of Field Names.

7. Click on **STREET** in the Field Names text box to highlight it.

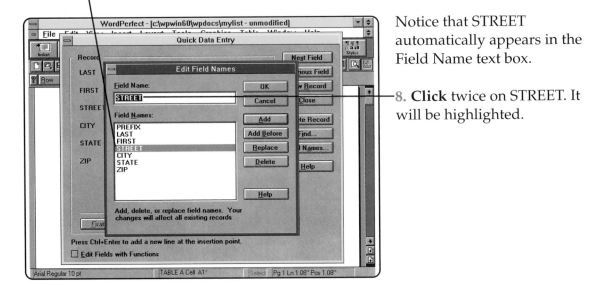

Notice that STREET automatically appears in the Field Name text box.

8. Click twice on STREET. It will be highlighted.

9. Type COMPANY. It will replace "STREET."

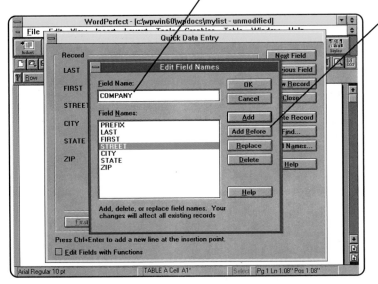

10. Click on **Add Before**. COMPANY will be inserted ahead of STREET in the list of field names.

11. Click on **OK**. The Quick Data Entry dialog box will appear.

Adding Data into the New Fields

Notice that the cursor is flashing in the PREFIX Record field.

1. Type Dr. in the PREFIX box. (Make sure your Caps Lock function is turned off.)

2. Press the **Tab key** three times to go to the COMPANY Record.

3. Type Creative Artists, Inc. in the COMPANY box.

4. Click on **Next**. A second Quick Data Entry screen will appear.

5. **Click** in the PREFIX box and **type Mr.**

6. **Press** the **Tab key** three times to reach the COMPANY box. (Or you can simply click on the box.)

7. **Type North Carolina Entertainment, Ltd.** in the COMPANY Record.

8. **Click** on **Close**. The Save changes to disk message box will appear.

9. **Click** on **Yes**. The MYLIST document will appear.

10 Click on **OK** to confirm that you want to save the file as mylist. Since "mylist" already exists, you will next be asked if you want to replace the existing file.

11. Click on **Yes** to replace the existing "myfile" with the edited version. The dialog boxes will close and you will be returned to the mylist table.

ADDING A NEW RECORD TO THE MAILING LIST

It is quick and easy to make additions to the mailing list.

Notice that the text in the COMPANY and CITY columns looks strange. Don't worry. You'll fix them later in this chapter.

1. Click on **Dr.** in the first cell of the table to place the cursor.

2. Click on **Quick Entry**. The Quick Data Entry dialog box will appear.

Notice that the first entry on the mailing list will appear. If you had clicked in another row on the table a different entry would appear.

3. Click on **New Record**. A second Quick Data Entry screen will appear.

Notice that the cursor is flashing in the PREFIX Record dialog box.

4. Type the following information in the Record dialog boxes (press Enter after each entry):

Ms.
Caldwell
Becky
Fancy Food and Fun
Corporation
812 Augusta Way
Cumberland
CO
54321

5. Click on **Close**. A Save changes to disk message will appear.

6. Click on **Yes**.

7. You will see the Save As dialog box. **Click** on **OK** to save this as mylist.

8. Click on **Yes** when WordPerfect asks if you want to replace the file.

CHANGING COLUMN WIDTHS IN THE MAILING LIST TABLE

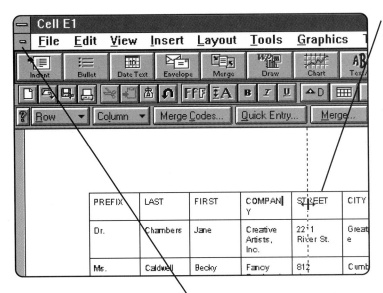

Sometimes a particular entry is too long for the column width that WordPerfect sets up. In this example you will change column width.

1. **Place** the mouse pointer on the column line after COMPANY. The pointer will change to a left-right arrow. You may have to fiddle with the pointer to get it to change to the right shape.

2. **Press and hold** the mouse button and **drag** the column divider to the right. When the column looks wide enough, release the mouse button. If the column isn't wide enough, repeat the process.

3. **Repeat steps 1 and 2** to increase the width of the STREET, CITY, and STATE columns.

4. **Press and hold** the **Ctrl key** and **type** the letter **s** (Ctrl +s) to save your work.

5. **Click twice** on the Control menu box (⊟) on the left of the menu bar to close the file.

Setting Up a Form Letter for Merge Printing

In Chapter 13 you completed your mailing list by adding new fields and data. You are now ready to code the letter to match the mailing list so that it will print personalized letters correctly. In this chapter you will do the following:

❖ Insert merge fields into a form letter

OPENING A LIST OF FIELD NAMES

1. Open the **preview.wpd** document that you created in Chapters 1-10.

2. Click on **Merge** in the button bar. The Merge dialog box will appear.

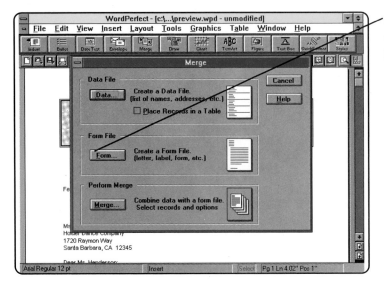

3. Click on **Form**. The Create Merge File dialog box will appear.

4 Click on **Use File in Active Window** to place a dot in the circle if it does not already have one.

5. Click on **OK**. The Create Form File dialog box will appear.

6. Click on **Associate a Data File** to place a dot in it if it does not already have one.

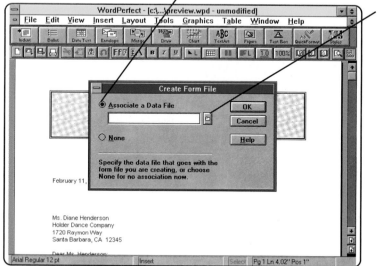

7. Click on the button to the right of the blank text box. The Select File dialog box will appear.

8. Click on mylist to highlight it.

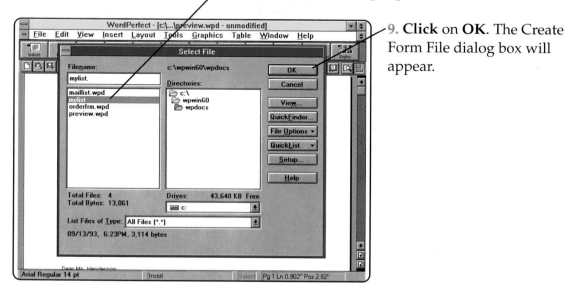

9. Click on **OK**. The Create Form File dialog box will appear.

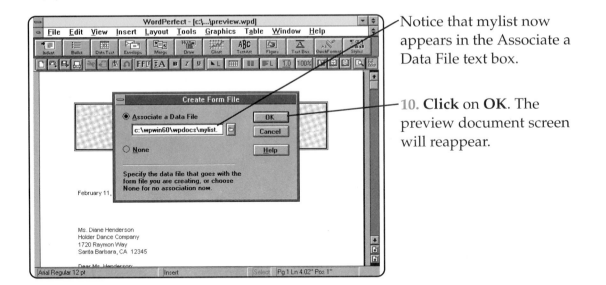

Notice that mylist now appears in the Associate a Data File text box.

10. Click on **OK**. The preview document screen will reappear.

INSERTING MERGE FIELDS INTO A FORM LETTER

Setting up the Address

1. **Drag** the **scroll bar button** so you can see the inside address of the letter.

2. **Click** to the **left** of the first line in the mailing address to set the cursor.

3. **Press and hold** the mouse button as you **drag** it down to **highlight the entire address**. **Release** the mouse button.

4. **Press** the **Backspace key** to delete the address. The cursor will be flashing in the space where the word "Ms." was located.

5. Click on **Insert Field** in the Merge feature bar. The Select Field Name or Number dialog box will appear.

6. Click and hold on the title bar of the dialog box and **drag** the dialog box to the bottom of the screen. This will allow you to see what happens next.

7. Click on **PREFIX**.

8. Click on **Insert**. "FIELD(PREFIX)" will appear in red on the first line of the address.

9. Press the **Spacebar** once to insert a space after the PREFIX field.

10. Click on **FIRST**.

11. Click on **Insert**. "FIELD(FIRST)" will appear after the "FIELD(PREFIX)" on the first line of the address.

12. Press the **Spacebar** to insert a space after the FIRST field.

13. Click on **LAST**.

14. Click on **Insert**.

If you goof and put a merge field in the wrong place, highlight it and delete it. Then repeat steps 5 and 6 to replace it with the correct merge field.

15. Press the **Enter key** on your keyboard to move to the next line in the letter.

16. Click on the ⬇ to scroll to the bottom of the Select Field Names box so you can see ZIP at the bottom of the list.

17. Enter the following words (field names) in the mailing address area of the letter:

COMPANY
STREET
CITY, STATE ZIP

Press the Enter key at the end of each line. Insert a comma and a space after "FIELD(CITY)." Put two spaces between the STATE and ZIP fields.

SETTING UP THE SALUTATION

1. Click to the **left** of **"Ms. Henderson"** to set the cursor.

2. Press and hold the mouse button as you **drag** the highlight bar over the **name. Release** the mouse button. Be careful not to highlight the colon.

3. Press the **Backspace key** to delete the prefix and name.

4. Repeat steps 5 and 6 in the previous section to add the following two fields to the salutation:

PREFIX

LAST

Remember to press the Spacebar between the PREFIX and LAST fields.

SETTING UP THE BODY TEXT

1. Click repeatedly on the ⬇ on the scroll bar until you can see the double line indicating the page break.

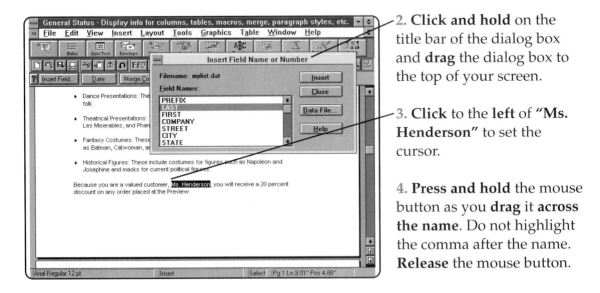

2. Click and hold on the title bar of the dialog box and **drag** the dialog box to the top of your screen.

3. Click to the **left** of **"Ms. Henderson"** to set the cursor.

4. Press and hold the mouse button as you **drag** it **across the name**. Do not highlight the comma after the name. **Release** the mouse button.

5. Press the **Backspace key** to delete the prefix and name.

6. Repeat steps 5 and 6 in the section entitled "Inserting Merge Fields in a Letter" to insert the following two fields (don't forget to press the Spacebar between PREFIX and LAST):

PREFIX
LAST

7. Click on **Close**.

COPYING AND PASTING MERGE FIELDS

You can use the Copy and Paste feature to copy the merge fields from the mailing address on Page 1 to page 2.

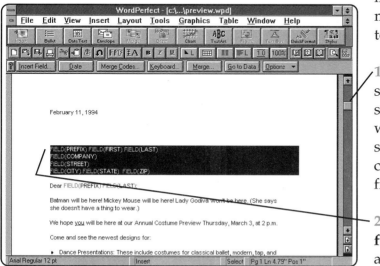

1. Click and hold on the scroll bar button and **drag** it so that it is about 1/5 of the way from the top of the scroll bar. Place it so you can see the inside address field codes.

2. Click to the **left** of the **first line** in the mailing address.

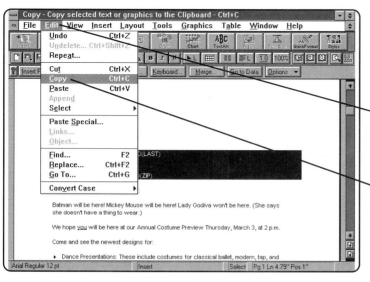

3. Press and hold the mouse button and **drag** the highlight bar **over** the **four lines of code**.

4. Click on **Edit** in the menu bar. A pull-down menu will appear.

5. Click on **Copy**. These lines are now copied to the buffer, a temporary storage area in your computer's memory.

6. **Press** the **Ctrl key** and the **End key** (Ctrl + End) to go to the end of the file.

7. **Click** to the **left** of **"Ms. Diane Henderson."**

8. **Press and hold** the mouse button and **drag** the highlight bar over the **four lines of the address**.

9. **Click** on **Edit** in the menu bar. A pull-down menu will appear.

10. **Click** on **Paste**.

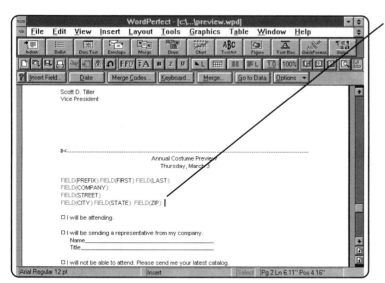

The copied fields will now be pasted into the document in place of the highlighted text.

INSERTING PERSONALIZED INFORMATION INTO A HEADER

1. Click to the **left** of the **name field codes** in the address you just pasted onto page 2.

2. Press and hold the mouse button as you **drag** the highlight bar over the **first line**. **Release** the mouse button.

3. Click on the **Copy button** on the power bar to copy the highlighted data.

4. Click on the ⬆ on the scroll bar to go up to the top of page 2.

WordPerfect - [c:\...\preview.wpd - H

File   Edit   View   Insert   Layout   Tools   Graphics

Indent   Bullet   Date Text   Envelope   Merge   Draw   Chart   TextA

Insert Field...   Date   Merge Codes...   Keyboard...   Merge...

Ms. Diane Henderson
February 11, 1994

Please return a copy of the reply form below by Wednesday, Feb

5. **Click** to the **left** of **Ms. Diane Henderson** in the header.

6. **Press and hold** the mouse button and **drag** the highlight bar over the name.

7. **Click** on the **Paste button** on the power bar to paste the codes for Ms. Diane Henderson into the header.

WordPerfect - [c:\...\preview.wpd - Header A]

File   Edit   View   Insert   Layout   Tools   Graphics   Table   Window   Help

Indent   Bullet   Date Text   Draw   Chart   TextArt   Figure   Text Box   QuickFormat   Styles

Insert Field...   Date   Merge Codes...   Keyboard...   Merge...   Go to Data   Options ▼

FIELD(PREFIX) FIELD(FIRST) FIELD(LAST)|
February 11, 1994

Please return a copy of the reply form below by Wednesday, February 23.

Sincerely,

Scott D. Tiller
Vice President

Arial Regular 12 pt   Insert   Select   Pg 2 Ln 1" Pos 4.34"

8. Click to the **left** of the **first line** of the letter to move the cursor out of the header field.

SAVING THE FORM LETTER WITH THE SAVE AS COMMAND

You can keep the original preview.wpd letter unchanged if you use the Save As command. This command allows you to give a new name to the changed version and keep the original letter unchanged.

1. Click on **File** in the menu bar. A pull-down menu will appear.

2. Click on **Save As**. The Save As dialog box will appear.

3. Type myform in the Filename text box. It will replace the highlighted preview.wpd that is there when this dialog box opens.

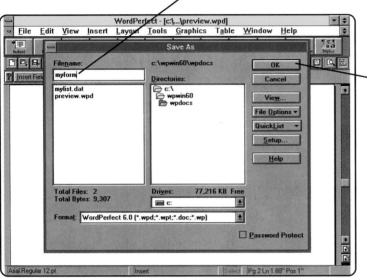

4. Click on **OK**.

You are now ready to merge print the form letter with the mailing list you created in chapters 11 and 12.

Printing a Form Letter

Now that you have finished coding the form letter in Chapter 14, you are ready to print it by merging the coded letter with the data file (the mailing list.) WordPerfect 6 will print as many personalized copies of the form letter as there are names on the mailing list. In this chapter you will do the following:

❖ Print three personalized copies of a form letter using a mailing list

SETTING UP TO PRINT A FORM LETTER

Although you can begin the merge printing process without having any files open on your screen, it's easier if you have the file you want to merge on your screen. Therefore, open the myform document if it is not already open. Press Ctrl + Home to go to the top of the file.

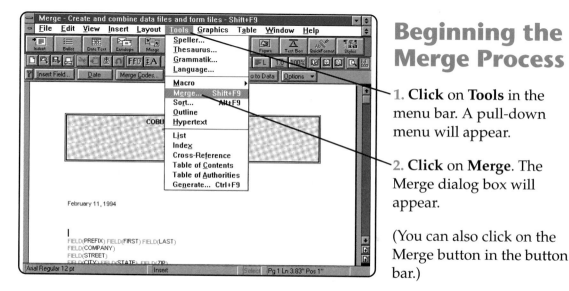

Beginning the Merge Process

1. **Click** on **Tools** in the menu bar. A pull-down menu will appear.

2. **Click** on **Merge**. The Merge dialog box will appear.

(You can also click on the Merge button in the button bar.)

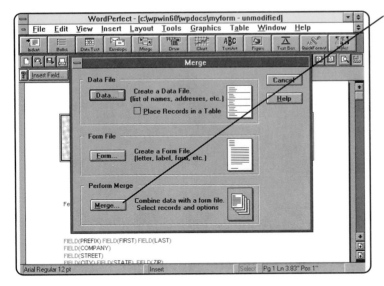

3. Click on **Merge**. The Perform Merge dialog box will appear.

SELECTING THE FORM FILE

Because you started the merge process with the coded form letter on your screen, WordPerfect has already identified the appropriate Form File.

1. Confirm that **<Current Document>** is in the Form File box.

SELECTING THE DATA FILE

Because you started the merge process with the coded form letter on your screen, WordPerfect knows which data file to use.

1. **Confirm** that **mylist** is the file listed in the Data File box.

PRINTING THE FORM LETTER

1. **Click** on the **button** to the **right** of the Output File text box. A menu will appear.

2. **Click** on **<Printer>**. <Printer> will appear in the Output File text box.

WordPerfect - [c:\wpwin60\wpdocs\myform - unmodified]

File Edit View Insert Layout Tools Graphics Table Window Help

Insert Field... Date Merge Codes... Keyboard... Merge... Go to Data Options

Perform Merge

Files to Merge

Form File: <Current Document>

Data File: C:\WPWIN60\WPDOCS\MYLIST.

Output File: <Printer>

OK

Cancel

Help

All Records

Reset Select Records... Envelopes... Options...

February 11, 1994

FIELD(PREFIX) FIELD(FIRST) FIELD(LAST)
FIELD(COMPANY)
FIELD(STREET)
FIELD(CITY) FIELD(STATE) FIELD(ZIP)

Arial Regular 12 pt Insert Select Pg 1 Ln 3.82" Pos 1"

3. **Click** on **OK**.

A "Please wait" message will appear briefly on your screen. WordPerfect will tell you which records are being merged (sent) to the printer.

After the form letters are printed, the original opening screen will appear. Do not close this file if you plan to go on to Chapter 16, "Printing Envelopes for a Mailing List."

4. **Click twice** on the **Control menu box** on the left of the menu bar to close the myform document. (Be careful not to click on the top Control menu box as this will close WordPerfect.)

Printing Envelopes for a Mailing List

Once you have created a mailing list (Chapter 12), you can print the entire list of envelopes from that file. The envelope form file can also be saved, used again, and attached to other mailing lists. In this chapter you will do the following:

❖ Set up an envelope to print from a mailing list
❖ Insert merge fields in the envelope's mailing address
❖ Print envelopes from the mailing list
❖ Save the envelope form file

SETTING UP AN ENVELOPE TO PRINT FROM A MAILING LIST

In order to print envelopes from a mailing list, you must first set up a special merge envelope just as you set up the form letter in Chapter 14. Open a new document file if one is not already on your screen.

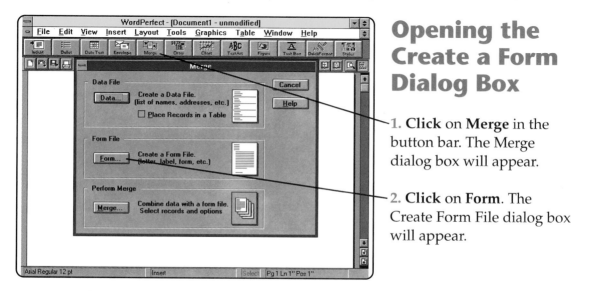

Opening the Create a Form Dialog Box

1. **Click** on **Merge** in the button bar. The Merge dialog box will appear.

2. **Click** on **Form**. The Create Form File dialog box will appear.

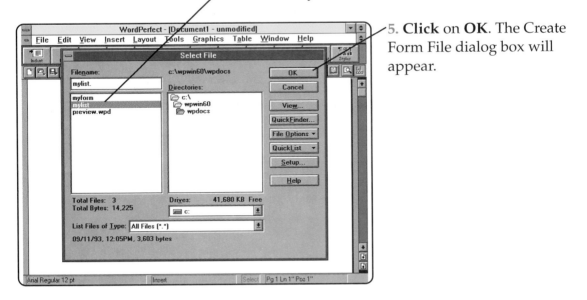

3. Click on the **button** to the **right** of the Associate a Data File text box. The Select File dialog box will appear.

4. Click on **mylist**.

5. Click on **OK**. The Create Form File dialog box will appear.

Notice that the file you selected appears in the Associate a Data File text box.

6. Click on **OK**. The document screen will reappear with the merge button bar.

OPENING THE ENVELOPE DIALOG BOX

1. Click on the **Envelope button** in the button bar. The Envelope dialog box will appear.

Inserting Merge Fields in the Envelope's Mailing Address

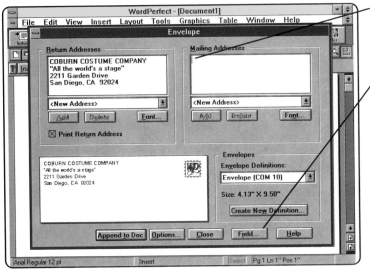

Notice that the cursor is flashing in the Mailing Addresses text box.

1. Click on **Field**. The Insert Field Name or Number text box will appear.

2. Click on the field **PREFIX** if it is not already highlighted.

3. Click on **Insert**. The Insert Field Name or Number dialog will disappear.

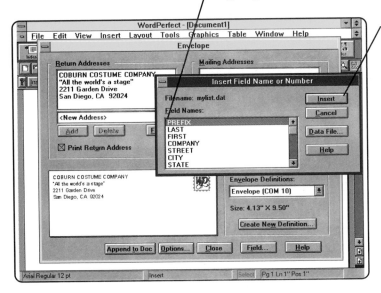

Notice that the cursor is flashing in the Mailing Addresses text box.

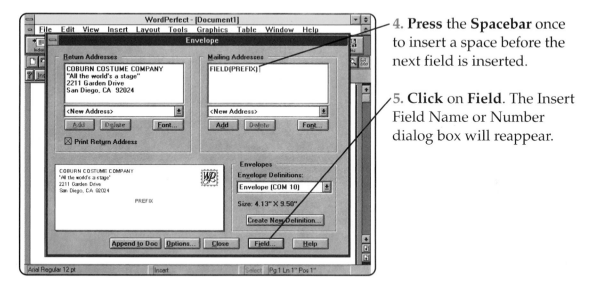

4. Press the **Spacebar** once to insert a space before the next field is inserted.

5. Click on **Field**. The Insert Field Name or Number dialog box will reappear.

6. Click on the field **FIRST**.

7. Click on **Insert**. The Insert Field Name or Number text box will close once again.

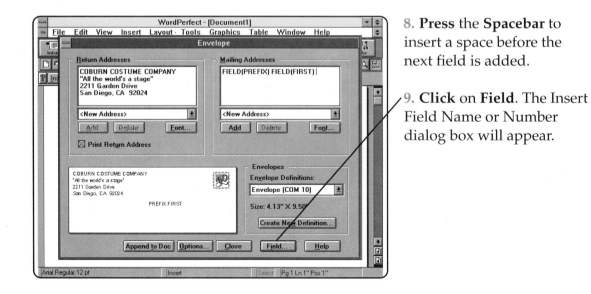

8. Press the **Spacebar** to insert a space before the next field is added.

9. Click on **Field**. The Insert Field Name or Number dialog box will appear.

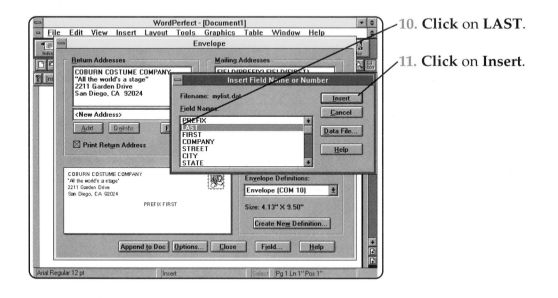

10. Click on **LAST**.

11. Click on **Insert**.

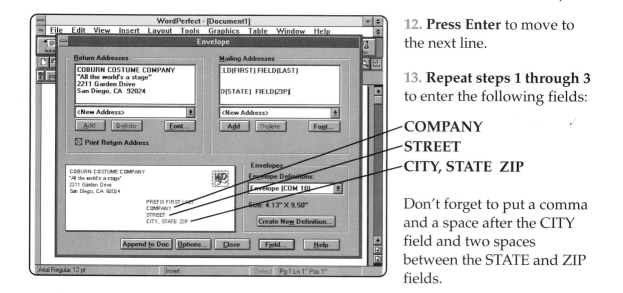

12. Press Enter to move to the next line.

13. Repeat steps 1 through 3 to enter the following fields:

COMPANY
STREET
CITY, STATE ZIP

Don't forget to put a comma and a space after the CITY field and two spaces between the STATE and ZIP fields.

Note: If you want to edit the Mailing Addresses text box use the arrow keys on your keyboard to make any changes.

CREATING THE ENVELOPE FORM FILE

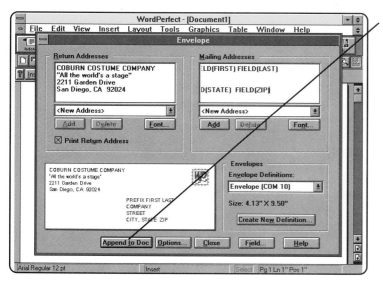

1. Click on **Append to Doc.**

PRINTING ENVELOPES FROM THE MAILING LIST

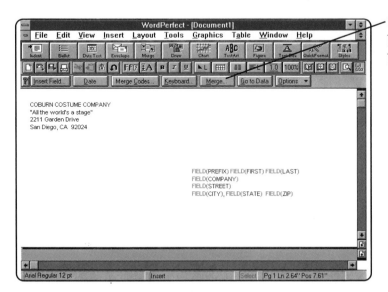

1. Click on **Merge** in the button bar. A Merge dialog box will appear.

2. Click on **Merge**. The Perform Merge Dialog box will appear.

3. **Click** on the **button** to the **right** of the Output File (<New document>) text box. A quick menu will appear.

4. **Click** on **<Printer>**. <Printer> will appear in the text box.

5. **Click** on **OK**. The Please Wait Merge Record message box will appear and flash as records are sent to the printer.

SAVING THE ENVELOPE

The envelope you created for mail merge may be saved for future use. It may be used with the file you just printed or attached to another WordPerfect mailing list.

1. **Click** on **File** in the menu bar. A pull-down menu will appear.

2. **Click** on **Save As**. The Save As dialog box will appear.

3. **Type myenvlop** in the Filename text box.

4. **Click** on **OK**.

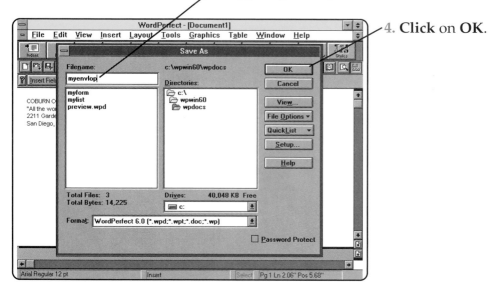

CLOSING THE ENVELOPE FILE

1. **Click** on **File** in the menu bar. A pull-down menu will appear.

2. **Click** on **Close**. The file will close.

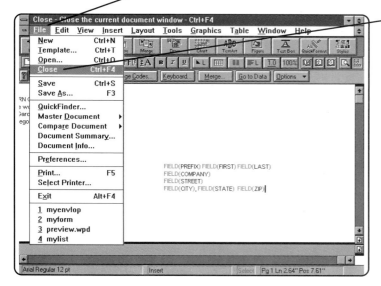

Converting a Mailing List

If you have a mailing list created in another word-processing program, you can easily convert the mailing list into a WordPerfect 6 file. In this chapter you will do the following:

❖ Convert a mailing list from another DOS-based program or from a windows-based program

❖ Add field names to the converted mailing list

❖ Save the mailing list as a WordPerfect data file

CONVERTING A MAILING LIST

Although this example shows an empty document screen, you can open a new file at any time. WordPerfect allows you to have multiple files open at the same time.

1. Click on **File** in the menu bar. A pull-down menu will appear.

2. Click on **Open**. The Open File dialog box will appear.

If you see only files with the .wpd extension in the Filename list, complete steps 3 to 5 so you can open documents with other extensions.

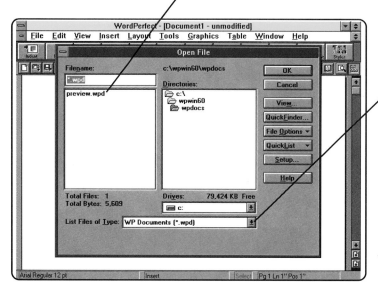

If the List Files of Type box shows all Files (*.*), go to step 6.

3. Click on the ↓ to the **right** of the List files of Type text box. A drop down list of file types will appear.

4. Click on the ↑ on the scroll bar so you can see **All Files (*.*)**.

5. Click twice on **All Files (*.*)**. All files in the directory, regardless of the extension, will appear in the Filename list box.

6. **Click** on the **Filename** of the file you want to convert. (In this example it is maillist.txt. This example assumes the original data file was moved to the WPDOCS.)

7. **Click** on **OK**. The Convert File Format dialog box will appear.

Notice that the path of the file to be converted appears in the file text box.

WordPerfect will identify the format of the original file. In this example the format of the file MAILLIST.TXT is ASCII Text.

8. **Click** on **OK**. A message box saying, "Conversion in progress," will flash on your screen. Then the list will appear.

CHANGING THE VIEW

It is easier to edit a mailing list if all of the information for each record is on one line. So, before you add field names to the file, you can change the view by making the font size smaller.

1. **Click** to the **left** of the **first row** to set the cursor.

2. **Press and hold** the mouse button as you **drag** the highlight bar over the **entire mailing list**. **Release** the mouse button.

3. **Click** on **Layout** in the menu bar. A pull-down menu will appear.

4. **Click** on **Font**. The Font dialog box will appear.

5. **Click** on **Arial** if it is not already highlighted.

6. **Click twice** on **10**. (That's the same thing as clicking once on 10 then clicking on OK.) The font size will change to 10 point and each record will now appear on one line.

ADDING FIELD NAMES TO A CONVERTED MAILING LIST

Entering Field Names

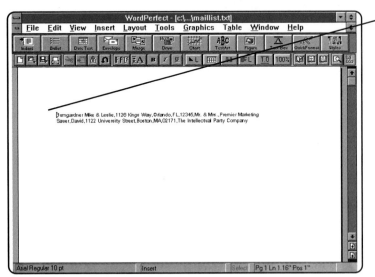

1. Click to the **left** of the **first line** to set the cursor.

2. Press the **Enter key** on your keyboard. The first line of text will move down one line. There will be an empty line above it.

3. Press the ↑ key on your keyboard to place the cursor at the beginning of the first row.

4. Type the following words (field names) on one line. Put a comma after each word. *But do not put a space after the comma* or this mailing list will not merge print correctly. Do not put a comma after the last field name. You can type field names in upper- or lowercase letters. WordPerfect will accept either.

LAST,FIRST,STREET, CITY,STATE,ZIP, PREFIX,COMPANY

SAVING THE MAILING LIST AS A WORDPERFECT DATA FILE

1. Click on **File** in the main menu. A drop-down list will appear.

2. Click on **Save As**. The Save As dialog box will appear.

3. Confirm that **WordPerfect 6.0 (*.wpd,*.wpt,*.doc,*.wp)** is in the Format box.

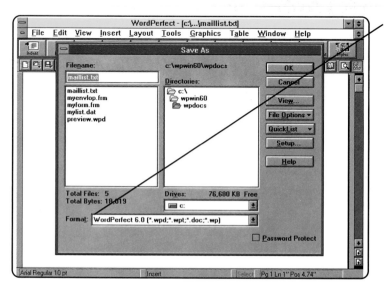

4. Click to the **left** of **".txt"** to set the insertion point.

5. Press and hold the mouse button as you **drag** the cursor to highlight **".txt"**. Be careful to highlight the period between maillist and txt.

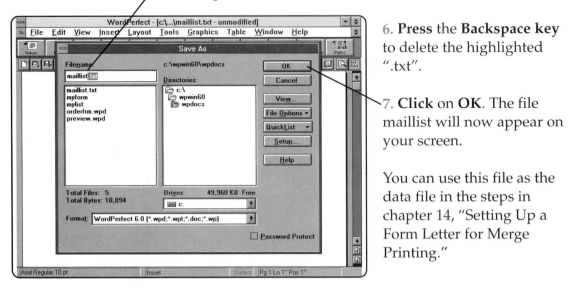

6. Press the **Backspace key** to delete the highlighted ".txt".

7. Click on **OK**. The file maillist will now appear on your screen.

You can use this file as the data file in the steps in chapter 14, "Setting Up a Form Letter for Merge Printing."

CLOSING THE FILE

1. Click twice on the **Control Menu Box** on the left of the menu bar. The file will close and you will have a blank document file on your screen. (Be careful not to click on the Control menu box above. Clicking twice on this Control menu box will close WordPerfect.)

Program Manager

Part IV Introducing Tables

Creating a Table

The tables feature in WordPerfect 6 makes it easy to organize information into columns and rows. Once the table is created, it operates like a basic spreadsheet. For example, you can join cells in the table to make room for a heading, increase the number of lines in a cell for a large entry, and increase or decrease the width of a column. You can even enter a formula into a cell and copy that formula to adjacent cells and sort data within a row or column. In this chapter you will do the following:

❖ Create a table

❖ Join cells

❖ Enter text and numbers

CREATING A TABLE

In this example you will create a table that has four columns and six rows. Although you can insert a table anywhere in an existing document, in this example you will open a new document for the table if you do not already have a blank document on your screen.

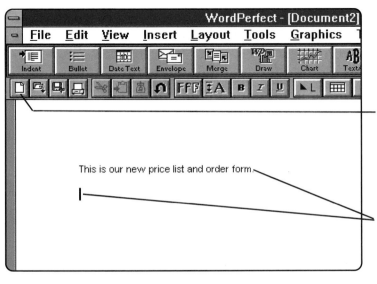

1. Click on the **New Document button** in the power bar. A blank document will appear on your screen.

2. Type the sentence **This is our new price list and order form.** Then **press Enter twice.**

Table Quick Create - Click and drag to create a table

File Edit View Insert Layout Tools Graphics Table

Indent Bullet Date Text Envelope Merge Draw Chart TextArt Fig

This is our new price list and order form

3. Place your **cursor** on the **Table button** in the power bar.

WordPerfect - [Document2]

File Edit View Insert Layout Tools Graphics Table

Indent Bullet Date Text Envelope Merge Draw Chart TextArt Fig

4x6

This is our new price list and order form

4. Press and hold your mouse button and **drag** your pointer until you have **highlighted 4 columns and 6 rows**. (The button will show 4 × 6 at the top of the diagram.)

5. Release your mouse button. The Table button will disappear and a table will appear in your document.

You can also create a table by clicking on Table in the menu bar then clicking on Create in the pull-down menu. But it's not nearly as much fun as using the Table button.

Notice that the cursor is flashing in the table and the status bar shows it is in Table A Cell A1.

This is Table A because it is the first table in the document.

The columns are referred to as A through D. The rows are labeled 1 through 6. The intersection of each column and row creates a cell. The cells are referred to as A1 through D6.

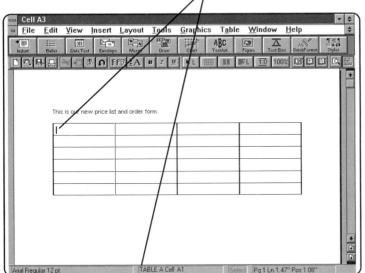

JOINING CELLS

When you join cells you remove the dividing lines between them to create a single, larger cell. In this section you will join the cells in the first row to create a single cell for a heading.

1. **Click** in cell **A1** to place the cursor if it is not already there.

2. **Press and hold** the mouse button and **drag** the highlight bar across the **first row** of the table to D1.

You will notice that the mouse pointer changes shape with annoying frequency when you work with tables.

3. Click your **right mouse button**. A quick menu will appear. (Quick menus are available throughout WordPerfect, not just in tables.)

4. Click on **Join Cells**. The dividing lines will be removed from the first row of cells.

ENTERING TEXT AND NUMBERS IN A TABLE

You enter and edit text in a table just as you would in the document itself.

1. Click on the **first row** in the table (Cell A1) if your cursor is not already there.

2. Type Coburn Costume Company.

3. Press Enter. This will add a line to the cell you are in.

4. Type Costume Order Form.

5. Press the **Tab key** on your keyboard. This will move you to the next cell, A2.

6. Type Costume and **press** the **Tab key**. The cursor will move to the next cell (B2). If you accidentally press Enter, an extra line will be added to the cell. Simply press Backspace and the extra line will be deleted.

7. Type Price and **press** the **Tab key**. The cursor will move to the next cell (**B3**).

8. Type Quantity and **press** the **Tab key**. The cursor will move to the next cell (**B4**).

9. Type Total and **press** the **Tab key**. The cursor will move to the next cell (**C1**).

10. Type Mickey Mouse in **C1** and **press Tab** to move the cursor to the next cell (**C2**).

11. Type 75 and **tab** to the next cell (**C3**).

12. Type 10 and **press** the **Tab key twice** to move to cell **A4**.

13. Type Catwoman and **tab** to the next cell (**B4**).

14. Type 95 and **tab** to the next cell (**C4**).

15. Type 5 and **press** the **Tab key twice** to move to cell **A5**.

Your table will look like the example to the left.

```
WordPerfect - [Document2]
File  Edit  View  Insert  Layout  Tools  Graphics  Table  Window  Help
```

This is our new price list and order form

Coburn Costume Company Costume Order Form			
Costume	Price	Quantity	Total
Mickey Mouse	75	10	
Catwoman	95	5	

Arial Regular 12 pt   TABLE A Cell A5   Select   Pg 1 Ln 2.92" Pos 1.08"

16. Type Phantom Mask and **tab** to **B5**.

17. Type 9.95 and **tab** to **C5**.

18. Type 12.

```
Cell A3
File  Edit  View  Insert  Layout  Tools  Graphics  Table  Window  Help
```

This is our new price list and order form

Coburn Costume Company Costume Order Form			
Costume	Price	Quantity	Total
Mickey Mouse	75	10	
Catwoman	95	5	
Phantom Mask	9.95	12	

Arial Regular 12 pt   TABLE A Cell C5   Select   Pg 1 Ln 2.92" Pos 4.52"

19. Click on **A6** and **type Totals**. (You can move through the table with the tab key, the arrow keys on your keyboard, or simply by clicking on the cell you want.)

Your screen will look like the example to the left.

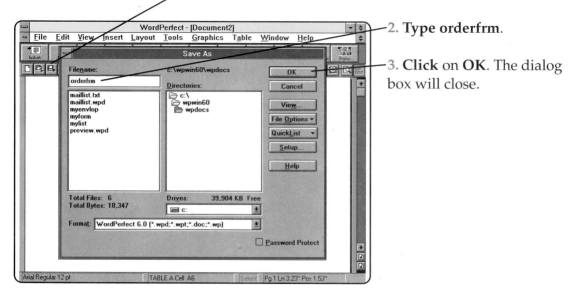

SAVING THE TABLE

1. Click on the **Save button** in the power bar. The Save As dialog box will appear.

2. Type orderfrm.

3. Click on **OK**. The dialog box will close.

Editing a Table

Once you have created a table, you enter and edit text and numbers as you would in the document itself. You can sort data in a table (or in a letter) alphabetically and numerically. You can add and delete rows and columns with ease. You can also remove the grid lines from the table. In this chapter you will do the following:

❖ Sort data alphabetically
❖ Sort data numerically
❖ Add a row to a table
❖ Delete a row from a table
❖ Change column widths
❖ Change the position of a table so that it is centered across the page
❖ Remove the grid lines from the table

SORTING DATA ALPHABETICALLY

You can sort data in a document and in a table. In this example you will sort the data in rows 3 through 5 alphabetically by the first cell in each row. Because you do not want to sort the entire table, you will highlight the rows you want to sort. Open orderform.wpd if it is not already open.

1. Click to the **left** of **Mickey Mouse** in cell A3 to place the cursor. Make sure your pointer is an I-beam.

2. Press and hold the mouse button and **drag** the highlight bar down to **D5**. The pointer will change to a left arrow as you drag.

This is our new price list and order form.

Coburn Costume Company Costume Order Form			
Costume	Price	Quantity	Total
Mickey Mouse	75	10	
Catwoman	95	5	
Phantom Mask	9.95	12	
Totals			

3. Click on **Tools** in the menu bar. A pull-down menu will appear.

4. Click on **Sort**. The Sort dialog box will appear.

In this example you will use the standard (default) sort settings.

Table Row is already selected as the Record Type because WordPerfect knows what you highlighted.

The Key definitions tell WordPerfect how to sort lines, as follows:

❶ **Key =1** means that you will sort on one criterion. You can sort on up to nine criteria. Consult *WordPerfect 6.0 Reference Manual* for directions on more complicated sorting procedures.

❷ **Type = Alpha** means this will be an alphabetic sort.

❸ **Sort Order = Ascending** means the sort is in ascending order (from A to Z).

❹ **Cell = 1** means WordPerfect will sort the lines based on the first cell in each line.

❺ **Line = 1** means the sort will be made on the first line in the cell.

❻ **Word = 1** means WordPerfect will sort on the first word in the cell. For example, in Phantom Mask the sort will be on "Phantom" rather than on "Mask."

5. **Click** on **OK** to start the sorting process. You will see a message box flash very briefly on your screen as WordPerfect sorts the data. When the sorting is finished, the data in the table will be rearranged on your screen based on the sort priorities you set in the Sort dialog box.

Your screen will look like this.

Pretty neat!

SORTING DATA NUMERICALLY

In this example you will sort the data in rows 3 through 5 based on the price of each costume.

1. Repeat steps 1 through 4 in the previous section to **highlight A3 through D5** and to **open** the **Sort dialog box**.

2. Click and hold on the **Type box**. A pull-down list will appear.

3. Continue to hold the mouse button and **drag** the **highlight bar** down to **Numeric**.

4. Release the mouse button. "Numeric" will appear in the Type box.

5. **Confirm** that **Ascending** is in the Sort Order box.

6. **Click twice** in the **Cell box** to highlight the number 1.

7. **Type 2** to tell WordPerfect to sort on the prices in the second cell in each row.

8. **Click** on **OK** to start the sorting process.

You will see the sorting message box flash briefly on your screen as WordPerfect sorts the data. When the sorting is finished, the data will be rearranged according to the price of the costumes.

Your screen will look like this.

UNDOING A SORT

You can undo a sort with the click of your mouse. But be sure *not to perform any other function* between the numeric sort and the Undo or else it won't work. In this example you will undo the numeric sort you just applied in the previous section and return to the alphabetic sort.

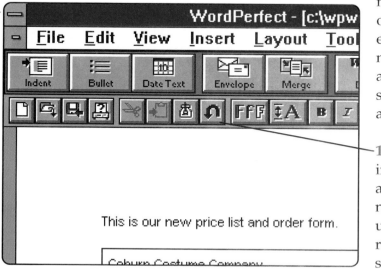

1. Click on the **Undo button** in the power bar. The last action you performed (the numeric sort) will be undone and you will be returned to the previous sort (the alphabetic sort).

ADDING A ROW (OR COLUMN)

You can add a row (or column) anywhere in the table. In this example you will add a row after row 3 using a quick menu.

1. Click on **Catwoman** in **row 3** to place the cursor.

2. Click the **right mouse button**. A quick menu will appear.

3. Click on **Insert**. The Insert Column/Rows dialog box will appear.

4. **Click** on **Rows** if it does not already have a dot in the circle. (You would click on Columns if you wanted to add a column to the table.)

Notice that you can add as many rows as you want by clicking on the ▲ to the right of the rows box. In this example you will add 1 row.

5. **Click** on **After** to insert a dot in the circle.

6. **Click** on **OK**. A row will be added to the table after row 3.

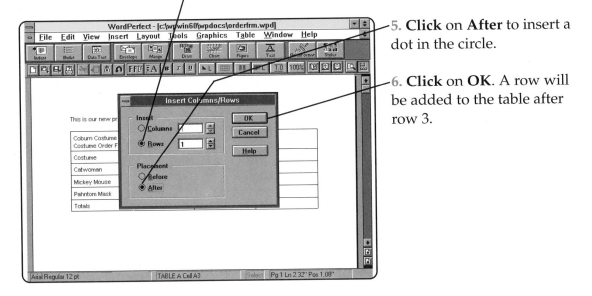

Your table will look like this.

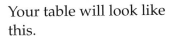

DELETING A ROW (OR COLUMN)

You can delete a row as easily as you added one. In this example you will use the Table pull-down menu to delete the row you just added.

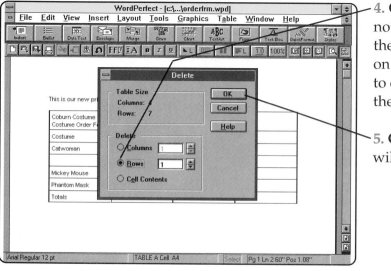

1. Click in the row you want to delete. In this example, click in the **new row** if your cursor is not already there.

2. Press the **right mouse button** to bring up the quick menu.

3. Click on **Delete**. The Delete dialog box will appear.

4. Click on **Rows** if it does not already have a dot in the circle. (You would click on Columns if you wanted to delete the column where the cursor is placed.)

5. Click on **OK**. The row will be deleted.

CHANGING COLUMN WIDTH

You'll be pleasantly surprised at the ease with which you can change column width. First, you will display the ruler bar.

1. Click anywhere in the **table**.

2. Click on **View** in the menu bar. A pull-down menu will appear.

3. Click on **Ruler Bar**. The ruler bar will appear on your screen.

If you do not see the column indicators (▼) on the ruler, click in any cell in the table.

4. Place the **mouse arrow** on top of the **indicator** for the **right edge** of the table.

5. Press and hold the mouse button and **drag** the dotted line to approximately **6¾ inch**.

6. Release your mouse button.

7. Repeat steps 4 through 6 to adjust the **second** and **third column** widths so that the last three columns are each about **1¼ inch wide**.

FORMATTING TEXT

You format text in a table just as you would any other text in a document.

1. Click outside the table **beside Coburn Costume Company**. The first line will be highlighted.

2. Click on the **Font Size button** in the power bar. A pull-down list will appear.

3. Click on **18**.

4. Repeat steps 1 through 3 to **change costume Order Form** to **14 point** type.

CENTERING TEXT

In this example you will highlight all of the cells in the first three rows, then center them all with one command.

1. Click outside the table **beside Coburn Costume Company**. (Make sure the mouse pointer is in the shape of an arrow.) The line will be highlighted.

2. With the mouse arrow in the left margin, **press and hold** the mouse button and **drag** the pointer down to **Costume** in row 2. All three lines of type will be highlighted. The shape of the mouse pointer will go through some strange changes from arrow to I-beam to the left arrow you see in the example.

3. Release the mouse button when you have highlighted the three lines of type.

4. Click and hold the mouse pointer on the **Alignment button** in the power bar. A pull-down menu will appear.

5. Continue to hold the mouse button and **drag** the **highlight bar** down to **Center**.

6. Release the mouse button.

7. Click anywhere on the document to remove the highlighting and the text will be centered.

CENTERING THE TABLE

When WordPerfect first creates a table, it extends the table the width of the page. When you change column width, WordPerfect keeps the same left margin. This often means that the table is no longer centered across the page. But you can center it very easily.

1. Click anywhere in the table if your cursor is not already there.

2. Click on **Table** in the menu bar. A pull-down menu will appear.

3. Click on **Format**. The Format dialog box will appear.

4. Click on **Table** to insert a dot in the circle. The dialog box will change to show options associated with a table.

5. Click and hold on **Left** in the Table Position box. A pop-up-list will appear.

6. Continue to hold the mouse button and **drag** the **highlight bar** to **Center**. Then release the mouse button.

7. Click on **OK**. The dialog box will close and your table will be centered across the page.

REMOVING THE RULER BAR

Since you will no longer need the ruler bar, you will remove it from your screen.

1. **Click** on **View** in the menu bar. A pull-down menu will appear.

2. **Click** on **Ruler Bar**. The pull-down menu will disappear and your ruler bar will no longer be visible.

REMOVING GRID LINES

You can remove the grid lines from a table. They will be removed from the screen and from the printed page.

1. **Click anywhere** in the table to place the cursor.

2. **Click** on **Table** in the menu bar. A pull-down menu will appear.

3. **Click** on **Lines/Fill**. The Lines/Fill dialog box will appear.

4. Click on **Table** to insert a dot in the circle. The dialog box will change to show options appropriate for tables.

5. Click on the ⬇ to the right of single. A pull-down list will appear.

6. Click on the ⬆ on the scroll bar to scroll up so you can see <None>.

7. Click on <None>.

8. Click on **OK** to close the dialog box. The table will appear with no grid lines. (You may see dotted grid lines on your screen. These dotted grid lines will not print.)

9. Click on the **Undo button** in the power bar to put the lines back in the table.

10. Click on the **Save button** on the power bar to save your work.

Formatting Numbers and Writing Formulas

You can format numbers to have decimal places, commas, dollar signs, and other characteristics. You can also write formulas in tables that will perform mathematical functions. In this chapter you will do the following:

❖ Change the format of numbers

❖ Change the alignment of numbers

❖ Write formulas for multiplication and addition

❖ Copy a formula to other cells

❖ Delete a table from a document

FORMATTING NUMBERS

In this example you will format the numbers in columns B and D as currency. You can format a single cell or the entire column.

1. **Click anywhere** in **column B**.

2. **Click** on **Table** in the menu bar. A pull-down menu will appear.

3. **Click** on **Number type**. The Number type dialog box will appear.

4. Click on **Column** to insert a dot in the circle. This will format the entire column rather than just the cell in which the cursor is located.

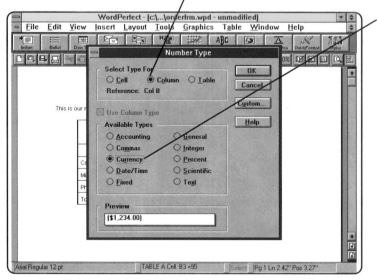

5. Click on **Currency** to insert a dot in the circle.

6. Click on **Custom**. The Customize Number Type dialog box will appear.

7. Click on **Use Currency Symbol** to *remove* the X from the box. When the X is removed, the $ will not print in front of each number.

8. Click on **OK** to close the dialog box. The Number Type dialog box will be on your screen.

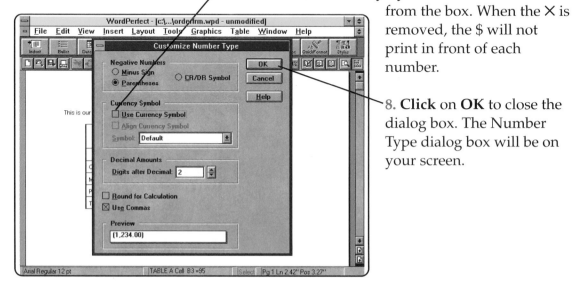

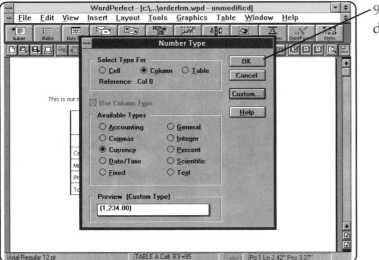

9. Click on **OK** to close this dialog box.

Notice that the numbers appear with two decimal places.

10. Click anywhere in **column D** to place the cursor.

11. Repeat steps 2 through 9 to format column D. You can format a column even when it is blank. Then, when you enter numbers into the column, they will appear in the specified format.

ALIGNING NUMBERS

In this example you will change the alignment of the numbers in columns B and D so that they are aligned at the right of the cell and the decimal places line up.

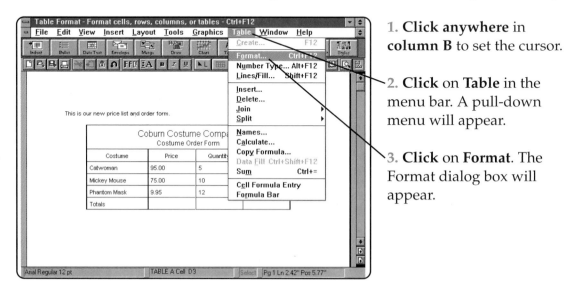

1. Click anywhere in **column B** to set the cursor.

2. Click on **Table** in the menu bar. A pull-down menu will appear.

3. Click on **Format**. The Format dialog box will appear.

4. Click on **Column** to insert a dot in the circle. The contents of the dialog box will change to options appropriate for columns.

5. Click and hold on **Left** in the Justification box. A pull-down list will appear.

6. Continue to hold the mouse button and **drag** the highlight bar down to **Decimal Align**. Release the mouse button.

7. Click on **OK** to close the dialog box.

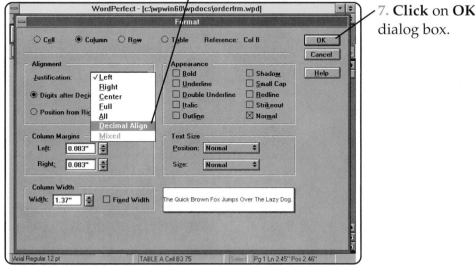

The numbers in column B will be aligned to the right at the decimal point.

8. Repeat steps 1 through 7 to align the numbers that will go into column D at the decimal point.

CENTERING NUMBERS

In this example you will use the Alignment button in the power bar to center the numbers in column C.

1. **Click** to the left of **5** in cell C3.

2. **Press and hold** the mouse button and **drag** the highlight bar down to **12** in cell C5.

3. **Click and hold** on the **Alignment button** in the power bar. A pull-down list will appear.

4. **Continue** to **hold** the mouse button and **drag** the highlight bar down to **Center**. Then release the mouse button.

Click anywhere in the document to remove the highlighting and see the centering.

WRITING FORMULAS

You can write formulas in your table that will perform mathematical functions. The most common functions and their symbols are as follows:

Function	Symbol	Example
Addition	+	D3+D4+D5
Subtraction	-	B4-C4
Multiplication	*	B3*C3
Division	/	B2/B3

Writing a Multiplication Formula

In this example you will write a formula to calculate the total in column D by multiplying the price in column B times the quantity in column C. You will write the formula for row 3, then later in the chapter you will copy the formula to rows 4 and 5.

1. Click on **D3**.

2. Click the **right** mouse button. A quick menu will appear.

3. Click on **Formula Bar**. A formula bar will appear on your screen below the power bar.

4. Click on **Functions** in the Formula button bar. The Table Functions dialog box will appear.

5. Click on the **first item** in the Function box.

6. Type pro. This will highlight the item PRODUCT (List).

7. Click on **Insert**. The Table Functions dialog box will disappear.

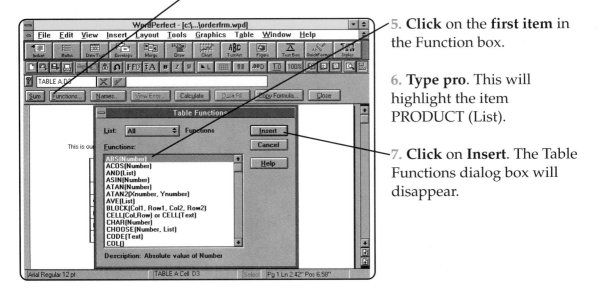

8. Type b3*c3. It will replace the highlighted text in the PRODUCT formula shown in the formula box.

9. Click on ✔ to the left of your formula. The number 475.00 will be entered into cell D3.

Copying a Formula

In this section you will copy the formula in D3 to D4 and D5.

1. Click in **D3** (475.00) if your cursor is not already there.

2. Click on the **Copy Formula button** in the formula bar. The Copy Formula dialog box will appear.

3. Click on **Down** to insert a dot into the circle.

4. Click on ▲ to make the number in the down box 2. This means the formula will be copied down two times.

5. Click on **OK**. The Copy Formula dialog box will disappear and the formula will be copied to D4 and D5.

USING THE SUM BUTTON

In this example you will sum the contents of D3, D4, and D5 using the Sum button in the formula bar.

1. **Click** on **D6** to place your cursor.

2. **Click** on the **Sum button** in the formula toolbar. The sum D3 through D5 (1,344.40) will be entered into D6.

3. **Click** on the **Close button** in the formula bar to close the formula bar.

DELETING AND UNDELETING A TABLE

Deleting and undeleting a table is as easy as deleting and undeleting text. In this example you will delete the table in the ORDERFRM document.

1. Place the mouse pointer in the **first cell** of the table so that it looks like the arrow you see in the example.

2. Press and hold the mouse button and **drag** the arrow down to the **last row**. The entire table will be highlighted.

3. Press the **Del key** on your keyboard. The Delete Table dialog box will appear.

4. Confirm that Entire Table has a dot in the circle.

5. Click on the **OK** to delete the table.

If you want to restore the table to your screen, click on the Undo button before you do anything else.

6. Click on the **Save button** in the power bar to save your work.

Program Manager

Part V Other Features

Using Quick Finder to Print Multiple Files

Using WordPerfect's Quick Finder makes printing multiple files a piece of cake. In this chapter you will do the following:

❖ Search for WordPerfect files in a specific date range
❖ Print Multiple files with one command

SEARCHING FOR FILES

There are a number of ways to search for specific files using Quick Finder. This example will illustrate searching for files in a specific date range. This example shows the search beginning from a blank screen but you can also use Quick Finder with a file open on your screen.

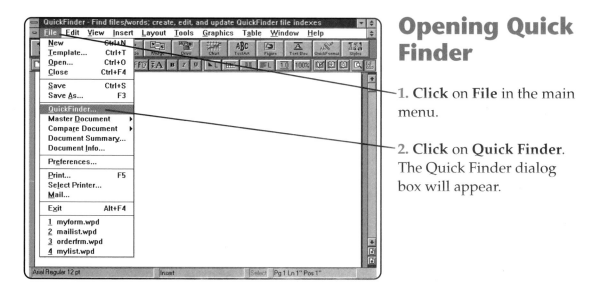

Opening Quick Finder

1. Click on **File** in the main menu.

2. Click on **Quick Finder**. The Quick Finder dialog box will appear.

3. Type *.wpd in the File Pattern text box.

Notice that c:\wpwin60 appears next to Directory in the Search In box. This means that the search will be done only in the wpwin60 directory. Because the files you have created in WordPerfect are stored in the wpdocs subdirectory, you want to change the search to include all subdirectories of wpwin60.

4. Press and hold on the ♦ to the right of the Search For button. A drop-down list of search options will appear.

5. Continue to **press and hold** the mouse button and **drag** the highlight bar down the list to Subtree.

6. Release the mouse button. The list will disappear and Subtree will appear on the Search In button. This tells WordPerfect to search all subdirectories of c:\wpwin60.

Selecting the Search Date Range

Notice that Subtree appears in the Search In button.

1. Click on the **button** to the **right** of the From Date Range text box. A pull-down calendar will appear.

2. Click on the **date** on which you want the search to begin. The calendar will disappear and the date you selected will appear in the From text box.

Clicking on the single arrow to the left and right of the month will move the month forward or backward. In this example, clicking on the single arrow to the left of September, 1993 will change the month to August, 1993. Clicking on the *double arrows* to the left and right of the month will change the year. In this example, clicking on the double arrow to the left of September, 1993 will change the date to September, 1992.

3. Click on the **button** to the **right** of the To Date Range text box. A pop-up calendar will appear.

4. Click on **Today**. The calendar will disappear and today's date will appear in the To text box.

5. Click on **WordPerfect Documents Only** to place an X in the box.

Starting the Search

1. Click on **Find**. The Search Results dialog box will appear.

In this example, Quick Finder will look in all the subdirectories of wpwin60 for all files with the extension .wpd that were created between September 3, 1993 and today.

PRINTING MULTIPLE FILES

If WordPerfect identifies a long list of tutorial lessons in the c:\wpwin60\learn subdirectory, click on the ⬇ on the scroll bar to bring preview.doc and orderfrm.doc into view.

1. Click on **orderfrm.wpd**.

2. Press and hold the **Shift key** and **click** on **preview.wpd**.

3. Click on **File options**. A drop-down list of options will appear.

4. Click on **Print**. The Print Files dialog box will appear.

5. Click on **Print**. Several printing message boxes will appear as the files are sent one by one to WordPerfect's print manager (spooler). Then, the WordPerfect Print Job dialog box will appear.

Notice that you can cancel a print job at any time by clicking on the Cancel Print Job button.

When the documents have finished printing the Search Results List dialog box will appear.

6. Click on **Close**. The WordPerfect document screen will appear.

Creating a Directory and Moving Files to the New Directory

WordPerfect has terrific file management capabilities. You can create directories and move and copy files without ever leaving WordPerfect! In this chapter you will do the following:

❖ Create a new directory

❖ Move two files to the newly created directory

CREATING A NEW DIRECTORY

WordPerfect is set up to store the files you create in the WPDOCS directory, which is a subdirectory of WPWIN60. As you create more and more files, you may find that you want to store all files of a certain type in a specific directory. For example, in this chapter you will create a special directory for your form letters.

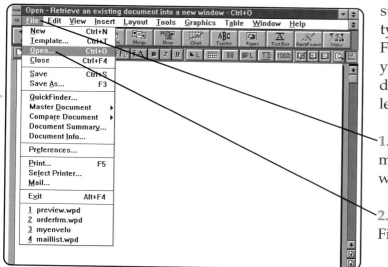

1. Click on **File** in the main menu. A pull-down menu will appear.

2. Click on **Open**. The Open File dialog box will appear.

3. Click on **File Options**. A pull-down menu will appear.

4. Click on **Create Directory**. The Create Directory dialog box will appear.

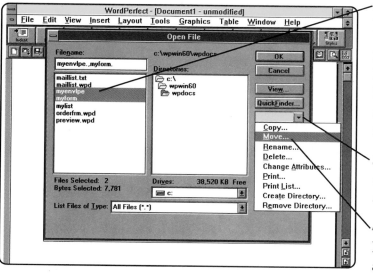

5. Type c:\wpwin60\ myforms. This will create myforms as a subdirectory of wpwin60 on C drive.

6. Click on **Create**. The Open File dialog box will appear.

Notice that the new directory does not show in the Directory list box because you are in the wpdocs subdirectory. However, you will see the new directory later in this chapter.

MOVING A FILE TO A NEW DIRECTORY

Open the Open File dialog box, if it is not already on your screen. (To open the Open File dialog box, go back and do steps 1 and 2 in the previous section.)

1. Click on **myenvlop** to highlight it.

2. Press and hold the mouse button and **drag** the highlight bar down to **myform**. Then **release** the mouse button.

3. Click on **File Options**. A drop-down menu will appear.

4. Click on **Move**. The Move File dialog box will appear.

5. Click on the **button** to the **right** of Move Selected File To list box. The Select Directory dialog box will appear.

6. Click twice on **wpwin60** in the Directories list box. The list of subdirectories of the wpwin60 directory will appear in the Directories list box.

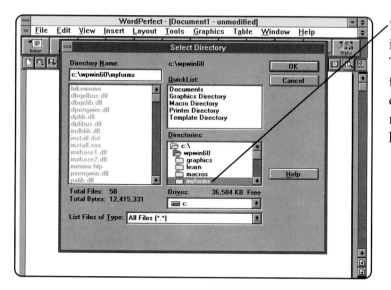

7. **Click twice** on **myforms** in the Directories list box. The list of subdirectories in the Directories list box will change and the subdirectory myforms will be highlighted.

Notice that only the myform subdirectory is listed.

8. **Click** on **OK**. The Move Files dialog box will appear.

9. Click on **Move**. The Open File dialog box will appear.

Notice that the files myenvlop and myform no longer appear in the File Name list box of the subdirectory wpdocs.

VIEWING THE MOVE

1. Click twice on **wpwin60** (the main directory for all WordPerfect files).

2. Click on **myforms**.

3. Click on **OK**. The list of subdirectories will change and only myforms will appear. The files you just moved will appear in the Filename list box.

Notice that myenvlop.frm and myform.frm now appear in the newly created myforms directory.

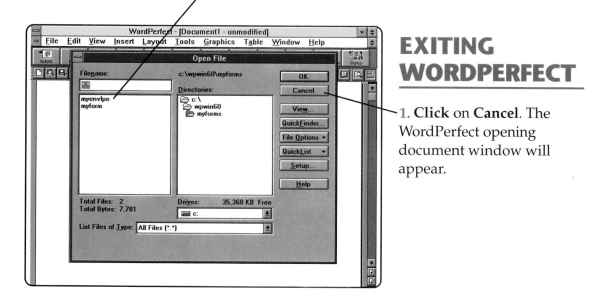

EXITING WORDPERFECT

1. Click on **Cancel**. The WordPerfect opening document window will appear.

2. **Click twice** on the **Control menu box** on the left of the WordPerfect title bar to exit WordPerfect. The Program Manager window will appear.

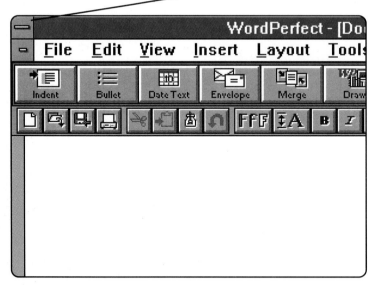

WHAT NEXT?

There are many exciting features of WordPerfect 6 left to explore. Creating a chart like the one shown here is just one of the options! We hope this introduction has given you an understanding of WordPerfect's capabilities. We hope, also, that you have gained confidence in your ability to master its complexities.

Experiment! Have fun!

Program Manager

Part VI Appendix

| Installing WordPerfect 6 for Windows | Page 247 |

Installing WordPerfect 6 for Windows

This appendix will describe a standard installation. If you want to customize your installation, refer to the *WordPerfect 6 for Windows Reference Manual*. In this appendix you will do the following:

❖ Install WordPerfect

Before you start, make sure that you have made and are using backup copies of your WordPerfect Install and Program disks. If you need help backing up your disks, see the *WordPerfect 6 for Windows Reference Manual*.

INSTALLING WORDPERFECT 6.0 FOR WINDOWS

1. **Open** Windows by **typing win** at the DOS prompt (C:\>). The Program Manager opening screen will appear. Your screen may look different from this one.

2. **Insert your backup copy of WordPerfect Disk Install disk 1** into drive A (or B).

3. **Click** on **File** in the menu bar. A pull-down menu will appear.

4. **Click** on **Run**. The Run dialog box will appear.

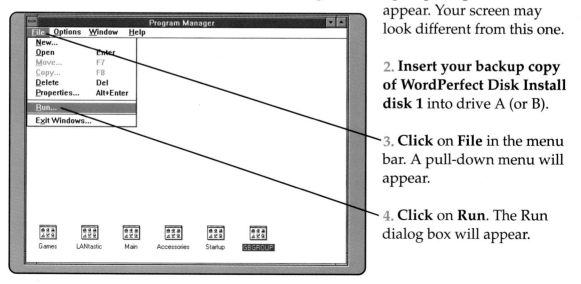

Notice that the cursor is flashing in the Command Line box. When you start typing, your text will be entered in the box.

5. Type a:\install (or b:\install).

6. Click on **OK.** The hourglass will briefly appear along with a WordPerfect message box that says, "Welcome to the WordPerfect 6.0 for Windows Installation Program" and "Copying work files." Next, the Registration Information dialog box will appear.

Notice that the cursor is flashing in the Name box. When you start typing, the cursor will disappear.

7. Type your **full name** in the Name box and then **press Tab** to move the cursor to the License number box.

8. If you have your license number handy **type** in your **license number.**

9. Click on **Continue.**

WordPerfect 6.0 for Windows Installation

Installation Type

Standard	Installs all WordPerfect for Windows (WPWin) files to a hard drive. Requires 31M of disk space.
Custom	Lets you customize the installation of WPWin.
Network	Required for installation on a network server or workstation.
Minimum	Installs the minimum number of files necessary for WPWin. Requires 14M of disk space.
Options	Lets you view README files, or install additional printers, language modules, or fonts.

Exit   Help

10. Click on **Standard**. After a pause the Select Drive dialog box will appear.

WordPerfect 6.0 for Windows Installation

Select Drive

Installing WPWin to drive: [c]
c:
d:

OK   Cancel

11. Click on **OK** since the C drive is already selected. (If you wish to install to another drive, simply click on that drive and then on OK.)

WordPerfect 6.0 for Windows Installation

If you're upgrading from a previous version of WordPerfect for DOS or WordPerfect for Windows, you can still use your previously created documents. The document conversion process is automatic--you can open a WordPerfect 5.1 or 5.2 document without going through any extra steps.

Install Files

Template Files

Cancel

Copying:	pressrel.wpt	
To:	c:\wpwin60\template\ ...	
This Disk:	85%	
All Disks:	5%	

At this point sit back and relax. As you install, watch the background information and pictures in the top half of your screen change as WordPerfect is copying the files from the disks to your hard drive. The Install Files dialog box will show you the percent of completion in copying files, both for the disk you are currently copying and as a percentage of all the disks.

After WordPerfect is done copying the files from the Install 1 disk, the New Diskette Needed dialog box will appear.

12. **Remove** the **Install 1 disk** from drive A and **insert** the **Install 2 disk**.

WordPerfect 6.0 for Windows Installation

With WPWin 6.0, you can see and edit your documents at any zoom setting from two full pages to 400 percent, complete with headers, footers, footnotes, endnotes, line numbering--in short, everything in the document, all on the same screen.

New Diskette Needed

Please insert the Install 2 diskette.

Diskette Location: a:\

OK   Cancel

Learning Files

Cancel

Copying:	less18.wpd	
To:	c:\wpwin60\learn\ ...	
This Disk:		
All Disks:	6%	

13. **Click** on **OK** or press Enter. The New Diskette Needed dialog box will disappear. WordPerfect will begin copying the files on Install 2.

Once again the Install files dialog box will appear and show you the percent of progress. WordPerfect will also continue to preview some of its features in the top portion of your screen as it is installing.

14. **Repeat steps 19 and 20 for the disks Install 3 through Install 6**.

You may get a message saying, "One or more install diskettes were not needed for this installation and have been skipped." (WordPerfect may not need Install 7, for instance.) Don't be concerned. WordPerfect is a "smart" program and will interact with your specific computer setup as necessary.

When WordPerfect is finished with the appropriate Install disks, the New Diskette Needed dialog box will appear and ask for the disk Program 1.

15. Repeat steps 19 and 20, but this time for the disks **Program 1 through Program 6**.

Towards the end of installing Program 6, you will see things happening as WordPerfect busies itself with the final stages of the installation. Don't worry! This means you are almost done. Finally the ReadMe Files dialog box will appear.

WordPerfect 6.0 for Windows Installation

Dive right in and make a splash with watermarks! You can now superimpose text over company logos and clip art images. Or choose one of the 30 commonly used phrases included with WPWin 6.0.

New Diskette Needed

Please insert the Program 1 diskette.

One or more install diskettes were not needed for this installation and have been skipped.

OK
Cancel
Help

Diskette Location: a:\

Copying: kickoff.exe
To: c:\wpc20\ ...
This Disk:
All Disks: 43%

WordPerfect 6.0 for Windows Installation

README Files contain information that was not available when program manuals and other documentation were printed.

Do you want to view the README Files?

Yes   No

16. Click on **No**. You will see another message box saying, "WordPerfect for Windows has been successfully installed!"

17. Click on **OK** in the WordPerfect for Windows Installation Complete message box.

Congratulations! You have successfully installed WordPerfect.

At this point you can go to the "Introduction" at the beginning of this book, select your first learning goal, and have fun.

In Chapter 1, "Changing Margins and Fonts and Entering Text," go to step 3 to start with a screen that looks like this one.

Index